HOSTAGE

A Police Approach to a Contemporary Crisis

HOSTAGE

A Police Approach
to a Contemporary Crisis

By

GEORGE F. MAHER
Assistant Chief Inspector
Nassau County Police Department
Mineola, New York

CHARLES C THOMAS · PUBLISHER
Springfield · Illinois · U.S.A.

Published and Distributed Throughout the World by
CHARLES C THOMAS • PUBLISHER
BANNERSTONE HOUSE
301-327 East Lawrence Avenue, Springfield, Illinois, U.S.A.

© *1977, by* CHARLES C THOMAS • PUBLISHER
ISBN 0-398-03698-5
Library of Congress Catalog Card Number: 77-9504

Printed in the United States of America
N-1

Library of Congress Cataloging in Publication Data

Maher, George F.
   Hostage.
    1. Hostages.   2. Abduction.   I. Title.
HV8058.M33   363.2'34   77-9504
ISBN   0-398-03698-5

PREFACE

THERE is a definite gap in the training of most law enforcement officers when it comes to the handling of the dynamic, emotionally-charged, and dangerous incidents involving people in crisis. Most agencies devote little, if any, time to the planning for a hostage/barricade/suicide situation, and, when it arises, there is usually chaos.

It would be presumptuous to state that this volume is *"The Training Manual"*; however, it should help the agency or individual officer in devising the necessary scheme of action to cope with the problem. After being in the business of tactical negotiating for about two years and receiving many inquiries on the subject, I wrote an article for a national police magazine on organizing a Hostage Negotiating Team. The article generated many more requests for information and convinced me that there was a need for a training manual that could be used in all agencies, regardless of size.

I do not attempt to give all the answers to the problems and, unlike other recently quoted "experts," offer no in-depth psychological profile for all persons who take hostages, become snipers, etc. This book should be recognized for what it is: an introduction to the problem for the uninitiated, a basis for further investigation of the subject, an outline for a training program, or a review of accepted techniques and procedures.

INTRODUCTION

THE HOSTAGE PROBLEM AND THE POLICE

THERE exists a relatively new problem facing the law enforcement community today that is slowly being recognized as a phenomenon requiring some in-depth consideration within the agency. The idea of taking a hostage to help achieve a particular goal probably started with early man, but it did not accelerate and gain world-wide interest until recent years. Hostages were taken in the past, but never on such a grand scale and not with so much nationwide publicity. What used to be mainly the tool of the terrorist has now become the means for many criminals and emotionally disturbed persons to achieve their desired effect no matter how bizarre it seems. A trapped criminal now has a recognized method of demanding the means to escape and is in some cases allowed to abscond after trading in one or more of the hostages. Emotionally disturbed persons demand all sorts of concessions from society as payment for sparing the life of the person being held. The police department that recognizes the problem for what it is, that is, a dynamic, dangerous occurrence, charged with emotion and considered to be highly newsworthy, is off on the right foot. The department that ignores the problem and figures that "it won't happen here" is in for a rude awakening when it does happen there. I do not advocate the formation of a special unit to deal with the hostage problem in every agency. However, I do recommend that every law enforcement organization, regardless of size, look into the problem, review the policies and procedures of the agencies that have dealt with these situations, and glean from them whatever can be used. If a department can afford the time and manpower, by all means it should train some people in the theory and tactics involved. Most of all, make sure that everyone responding to the scene knows the organization's policies and objectives and what is expected of the individual officer.

As the last pages of this volume are nearing completion, hostage and barricade situations seem to be happening with scheduled regularity across the country: Indianapolis, Indiana, where the media contributed to a circus atmosphere and then criticized law enforcement for not living up to a bargain that anyone with common sense knew could not be kept; New Rochelle, New York, where a crazed mass murderer exhausted the resources of a police department in a few bloody minutes; Warrensville Heights, Ohio, where a man with wild demands invaded the police station and held an officer hostage until the President of the United States became involved in the negotiation; Washington, D.C., where terrorists took and held hostages in a display of anarchy that shocked the American public.

In an attempt to keep a "handle" on these and other, not so newsworthy, incidents, members of the Nassau County Hostage Negotiating Team have been sent to various scenes while in progress and have interviewed officers who have been involved in others. Nothing the Team has discovered has in any way indicated that a change is necessary in the original policies and procedures outlined in this manual.

One thing is recognized, and that is that no firm guidelines can be established for dealing with a quasi-religious group of fanatics bent on large-scale terrorism. Unfortunately, a play-it-by-ear negotiating policy (with plenty of outside help) has to be accepted. I hope that most of the future hostage/barricade situations across the country are generated by the plain, ordinary, run-of-the-mill criminal or emotionally disturbed person so that some small spark kindled in the mind of a police officer, as a result of this book, can result in the saving of a life or freeing of a hostage.

CONTENTS

HOSTAGE

A Police Approach to a Contemporary Crisis

Chapter One THE POLICE
APPROACH TO A HOSTAGE SITUATION

IT IS 9:30 AM, Wednesday, September 14, in River City. The weather is sunny and warm, the children are all in school, and the early morning shoppers are starting to park along Main Street. An officer in a radio car has just called in and advised his dispatcher that he has completed school crossing duty and has received an O.K. to get some coffee. As he drives down Main Street toward his favorite restaurant, he hears a radio notification that the First National Bank silent alarm has been triggered. The bank is just a block away, so he speeds up and pulls to the curb in front of the building. As he opens the door and starts to exit the car, he sees two men start out of the front door of the bank. Both are wearing ski masks. As they spot him, one pulls a gun from under his jacket and fires a shot which shatters the rear window of the patrol car. The officer ducks behind the rear of the car and is about to return fire when the men duck back into the bank.

The officer keeps low and makes his way to the microphone. He calls his radio dispatcher and asks for immediate assistance, advising that he has been fired upon from the bank.

A Sergeant/Patrol Supervisor arrives on the scene in addition to other patrol units. He announces his location, clears a radio channel for the incident, and advises all units that his vehicle will be the command post for the time being. The Sergeant directs that specific units block traffic on Main Street a block away from either side of the bank. He assigns other units to take positions at the rear and sides of the bank building. A supermarket parking lot a block away is designated as a staging area for any other responding units. Stores across from the bank are evacuated through rear doors, and pedestrian traffic is eliminated.

The Sergeant notifies his dispatcher of the situation, requests hostage negotiators, and the precision firearms teams. Meanwhile, one of the subjects appears at the front door of the bank and, using a female as a shield, shouts that he will kill all of the bank employees and customers if the police try to enter the building. The Sergeant, using the designated radio frequency, advises all officers that no shots will be fired without orders.

The hostage negotiators arrive at the staging area at about the same time as the precision firearms teams and the Station Commander, a Captain. He confers with the first officer, the Sergeant, the negotiating team, and the sniper team and decides to establish a command post down the block from the bank in a drug store. Emergency equipment — ambulance, tear gas devices, and extra radios are ordered. The members of the firearms team are ordered to position themselves at locations surrounding the bank.

The negotiating team readies its recording equipment and prepares to call the bank by telephone. The Captain, meanwhile, has advised all officers that he is in command, has given the location of his command post, and has re-enforced firearms discipline. He ascertains that an inner and outer perimeter are established and all evacuation is complete and orders a withdrawal of all officers in the inner perimeter as the precision firearms teams take up positions. He designates a media liaison officer and notifies the dispatcher that all press inquiries shall be channeled through this officer at a point on the edge of the outer perimeter. The Captain makes sure that all officers are in clear communication with the command post and requests that the hostage negotiators begin to communicate with the subjects.

It sounds great, doesn't it, all the units of a good-sized department performing their functions according to the book. It has happened this way. Everyone did his job. The bank robbers were captured and the hostages freed unharmed. But, not every agency has the resources of "River City." If your department is smaller, does not have the equipment, or has not begun to plan for such an incident it really is not that important. The basic ideas put forth in this book will still work.

You, the first cop at the scene, may be the "negotiating team." A couple of off-duty officers with hunting rifles may turn out to be the "precision firearms team." Your boss, a Sergeant, may run the whole show. The local volunteer fire department may control traffic and establish perimeters. Or, your agency may call for outside help from county, state or federal agencies. Meanwhile, you should have some idea of the best way to approach this type of incident. In this book you will read about the recommended equipment and trained manpower that would be nice to have available. If you have it, use it correctly. But, if you don't have it, or it is going to take a while to get there, use your own common sense and, in most cases, a successful operation will result.

POLICY

You are an officer on patrol, and a radio call is received indicating that there is a stick-up in progress at a local bank. When you arrive at the scene, four apparently armed males are spotted in the bank. As you and other officers surround the bank and wait for them to leave, you find that each one of the robbers has taken a female employee and is forcing her to protect him as he exits the bank. Now what do you do? Or, you are called to a bridge; a young girl is in the center of the span threatening to jump. The bridge is about 100 feet over the water and you know that the fall will be fatal to her. Where do you start? Or, perhaps you receive a call to a house in a residential area, and when you arrive you are told by a woman that her son who is secreted in the attic of the home has a loaded rifle. He has threatened to kill himself if anybody starts up the stairs. What is your first move going to be? These situations are not unusual. Police officers throughout the country are expected to deal with this type of activity every day of the week. The officer of a department that is prepared to react professionally in each of the situations has a jump on any department that has no preplanned guidelines, leaving officers to figure out what to do after arrival at the scene. In preparing the personnel of a department for a hostage situation, a threatened suicide situation, or a barricaded, armed subject, there are a number of things that must be considered. One of the prime objectives of the agency must be the issuance of a clear policy/procedure to all members of the department. An agency policy that is given out once and forgotten has little value, and a written policy that is only distributed with the hope that most of the men will read it is also less than adequate. The ideal method is to issue a policy which is supported by the top-line management and administrative officers of the department. These officers, after being thoroughly familiarized with it by actually taking part in the formation of many of the items that make up the policy/procedure involved, will usually get the idea across to the rest of the department. The policy must not only cover what is expected of the first officer at the scene, but also the first supervising officer and the overall commander of the operation. The doctrine of the department in regard to vital questions must be clearly understood: Is the hostage's life of prime importance? Do we let the criminal escape in a trade-off for a hostage? Do we make concessions and promises that will not be kept? Policy questions such as these, plus the tactical approach to the situation, should be covered, with some special emphasis on media relationship. If the concept of negotiation is to be introduced, a policy/procedure that will fit the resources of the agency and be accepted by not only the members of the agency but also the general public is a necessary first step.*

POLICE RESPONSE TO A HOSTAGE/BARRICADE/SUICIDE SITUATION

The traditional police response to an incident in which a subject is "holed up" in a building, possibly firing into the street, or holding a hostage is usually counter fire with eventual assault. This is commonly done with or without chemical agents such as tear gas, and much noise, confusion, property damage, and sometimes injury or death result. In recent years, many departments have developed Special Weapons and Tactics (SWAT) teams which cut down on the confusion to some degree and, in addition to just ineffective counter fire by semi-trained officers, now react with selective sniper fire by experts (if they can see the subject). However, few departments in the past ever seriously attempted to contain and negotiate with the subject or subjects involved. Until

---

*See Appendix I for sample policy.

the Munich Olympic tragedy and other incidents throughout the world brought the hostage problem to the forefront and some agencies proved the value of actual down-to-earth negotiations, little was done in law enforcement circles to recognize and prepare for the problem. We all know the dangers involved in assaults. Unless there is a well-trained unit possessing the necessary equipment, with which they are thoroughly familiar, an assault on a building held by an armed subject can result in serious injury or death to the officers involved. Counter fire, in most cases, has proven to be not only ineffective, but highly dangerous. There are cases in which police officers have been wounded by the inaccurate, unnecessary counter fire of brother officers. This is not to say that in all cases an assault on the premises where a subject is barricaded or holding a hostage is out of the question. An assault team should always be available to back up the negotiators. If negotiations should break down and the hostages are in imminent danger of physical harm, there may be nothing left but an assault on the building. Selective sniper fire, a recent innovation, is of value. However, most small and medium size agencies have not been able to expend the man-hours involved in the necessary continuing practice. If the officers involved are not thoroughly trained, sniper fire can be highly dangerous to persons in the vicinity of the target. This capability should be used only as a last resort and when there is no other choice but to kill the subject involved. Naturally, it should only be done upon the command of the ranking officer at the scene, and all officers participating, particularly the negotiators, should have full knowledge of what is to happen. Any time authorized shots are to be fired, all officers at the scene must be alerted.

Chemical agents can be extremely hazardous to all occupants of the building where the subject is contained. Most of the common police-use chemical agents start fires. Many others are so potent that, when used in a closed room, they can actually result in the incapacitation or death of all the occupants of the room. Tear gas should not be considered unless the necessary back-up equipment is on the scene, such as gas masks, oxygen, and immediately available fire equipment. A less violent containment and negotiation technique should always be tried. Assault, sniper fire, and chemical agents can also be used after an attempt has been made to negotiate with the subject. The most important thing most officers can do at the scene is to *slow down*. Do not take action just for the sake of doing something. Attempt to calm any officer who is excited enough to react violently to what he believes is a hazardous situation. Think before acting; there is no rush, and time is usually on the side of the police. Some of these situations have lasted for days, even weeks. Sometimes initial thoughtless acts taken by the police first at the scene will hamper initial negotiations and may be very difficult to explain in any future negotiations. We can always escalate a situation, but it is very difficult to de-escalate. Once violent reaction to a subject has taken place, it is extremely difficult to get the idea across that we are on the path of nonviolence. Again, slow down!

SIMILARITY OF APPROACH

Most of the basic "street psychology" used to deal with a hostage situation can be used with a person attempting suicide or a subject barricaded alone in a building. Many times the holder of a hostage or a barricaded subject is involved in a bizarre attempt at suicide. Often the hostage holder is an emotionally disturbed person who, with or without the hostages, would possibly be in the same or a similar situation. The basic police approach to most situations should start out generally in the same tack. Surprisingly, many subjects are eager to capitulate and make the police look good, if the right approach is taken from the start. It is commonly accepted that if the person is yelling, even cursing the police, he can be talked to. The jumper probably would have jumped already, the hostages would be dead, and the barricaded person would have killed himself or others if the subject had a firm course of action planned. Police should not hesitate in using whatever expertise they have in crisis intervention, family disturbances, and generally dealing with excited persons when dealing with a hostage/barricade/suicide situation.

THE USE OF PSYCHOLOGICAL ASSISTANCE

There are many pros and cons on the subject of using professional psychiatrists or psychologists at the scene of an attempted suicide, hostage, or barricade (SHB) situation. However, the use of a professional psychologist in the training of a negotiating team is beyond question. Many clinical psychologists and psychiatrists may jump at the chance to become involved as a consultant to a police department engaged in this type of activity. However, many of these same professional people at the scene of a situation may not be of significant value in dealing with the subject. The identification and confrontation of a strange psychologist or a psychiatrist to the subject, who does not believe he has a mental problem, may turn him off and negate successful negotiations. He may be looking for a symbol of authority, such as a police officer, and would not welcome a doctor of any type. Indeed, most psychiatrists and psychologists will admit that they are not as effective in dealing with people in crisis situations as most police officers are. They say that it may take them months to size up a patient, find out exactly what is bothering him, and diagnose his condition before treating him; police officers usually react rapidly to crisis situations and are expected to deal with emotionally disturbed people in minutes. If the agency has available a psychologist or a psychiatrist who is thoroughly familiar with police policy and philosophy and knows what is expected of him at the scene, the depth of his involvement is something for the department to evaluate.

TYPES OF HOSTAGE SITUATIONS

For clarity we shall call the person who takes a hostage the "holder." There are four basic situations that the police are called upon to deal with. The first involves the criminal. We often become involved with the criminal when he is escaping from a crime, is confronted by the police, and takes a hostage to facilitate his escape. The second type, and the most common situation, involves the mentally disturbed person. He becomes a holder for many reasons. Various types of stress and anxiety produce reactions that are sometimes impossible to predict. Third, we have the unorganized group. These involve the typical jail riot or the unorganized crowd involved in a civil disturbance. The fourth, and fortunately the least common in the United States, is the radical or revolutionary organized group that takes one or more hostages to further its political aims.

Of the four types, the criminal is usually the easiest holder to deal with. He is accustomed to the police and we are used to him. He usually can predict what the police will do, and he knows what to expect if and when he is captured. He is aware of police limitations and relates to police actions. He usually understands how far the police can go in acquiescing to his demands. Most important, he also knows the effect on his status if the hostage is killed or injured. It most cases, all he wants to do is get away from where he is. However, he very often can be convinced that the best course of action is to simply give up.

On the other hand, the mentally disturbed person is usually the most difficult to deal with. If our easy-to-get-along-with criminal turns out to be a mental problem, the entire situation changes. The emotionally disturbed person can get himself into what may be a disguised suicide attempt, but he may be the type of individual who, although he wants to commit suicide, wants you to help him along. Most psychologists would agree that if the holder of a hostage, or the barricaded subject, is calm, cool, and collected; much less excited than you are; and seems to be enjoying himself, be careful. This is the type of person who will probably kill and usually is extremely difficult or impossible to negotiate with.

The third problem, the unorganized group who, for example, may be involved in a spontaneous riot and taking of hostages, is easier to deal with than the organized group provided rapid action is taken. Once a leader is chosen and a course of action accepted, this group becomes very difficult. Most jail procedures recommend rapid reaction to a disturbance, and their policies could limit concessions and in-depth negotiations for the release of hostages. The rule in most jails is that no prisoner will be allowed to escape from the institution because he is holding a jail employee as a hostage. Correction officers are aware of these rules and must be willing to live with them when applying for their jobs. Accordingly, seldom will a police hostage negotiating team be called in to deal with a jail riot or an attempted escape by inmates holding hostages. There are, however, "holding pens" or temporary detention facilities in many court houses, police stations, etc. where the possibility exists of police being called upon to deal with a group of prisoners holding hostages. It is generally believed that immediate action is the best action. These prisoners usually may be handled in the same way that any holder is handled who becomes such as a result of criminal activity. In many cases escape is not the prime demand made by the holders of correctional institution hostages. As a result, much of the negotiation would have to be handled by the officials of the correctional institution involved, who can intelligently deal with the demands laid down by the holders.

Dealing with an organized terrorist group by most local police agencies would be extremely difficult without outside assistance. Individuals who make up these groups, usually not common in the United States, are sometimes willing to die for their cause and take any and all hostages with them. The confrontation may be the result of months of planning, and all the alternatives and arguments put forth by the negotiators will have been considered and predicted by the group. A confrontation by police with such a group would be an unusual situation, and, for the most part, the political demands of the group probably would be above any concessions offered by local police. These groups usually do not want to talk to the police but would like a high-ranking official or representative of the media present at the scene to deal with them. Publicity is their bread and butter, and the more notoriety the incident can get, the better off they think their cause becomes. Our society will not permit dealing with terrorist groups in the way that they are handled in many foreign countries. Some Middle Eastern countries will not recognize that the life of a hostage is of primary importance so that, when hostages are taken, very often they are considered to be expendable and may be killed along with the holders during an assault. This is not generally acceptable in the United States, and terrorist groups are aware of it, so that it is not unreasonable to assume that there will be an increase in terrorist activities in our urban areas. Intelligence files should be kept on any militant quasi-terrorist group forming in the jurisdiction covered by the agency so that if the group becomes active and causes an incident, at least they can be identified and an attempt made to deal with them effectively from the point of view of negotiation.

No matter what type of hostage or barricade incident is being dealt with, the criminal, mentally disturbed person, or jail or terrorist group, the speedy development of intelligence and background information about the holder or holders is of primary importance. Usually no effective negotiation can take place without information about the subject. If the agency is fortunate enough to have a negotiating team call out procedure that will allow the response of four to five team members to each incident, the gathering of background information becomes somewhat easier. Members of the trained negotiating team who are assigned to gather intelligence will usually obtain more in-depth background information that can be used effectively in negotiation than officers who do not have negotiations in mind. Be careful of uncritical reliance on information received from relatives. There have been cases where a father and mother of a subject will paint a rosy picture about their misunderstood son, but when the estranged wife is interviewed, a totally different idea of the person being dealt with is evident. It is very difficult to make a judgment as to who to believe. Information regarding a hostage is also important, particularly if the hostage has any physical condition that will be aggravated by the situation he or she is now involved in. It is recommended that during negotiation little obvious attention be paid to the hostage by the negotiators. This is so that the importance of the hostage is not amplified in the eyes of the holder and also so that the hostage does not take the stage away from his captor. Be careful during a prolonged incident that the hostage does not shift sides, that is, become involved and sympathetic to the goals of the holder. This is not that uncommon, and there have been incidents where female hostages have become emotionally involved with the holder, probably due to a deep-seated feeling of thankfulness to the captor for not exercising the life and death power he has over the hostage during the time of confinement.

THEORY OF NEGOTIATION

The basic theory of negotiation for a hostage is simple. Try not to give anything without getting something in return. That is, negotiate for everything possible. Give up food, drink, cigarettes, comfort, etc. only for some concession on the part of the holder, such as the release of one or more of the hostages, removing a gun from the head of a hostage, allowing a doctor to treat the injured hostage, and so on. Never, never set a time limit on negotiation. Again, slow down! Time is on the side of the negotiator. In most cases, if there was going to be any injury to a hostage, it would have taken place already. The longer a hostage is held by the holder, the more difficult it becomes for the holder to kill or injure the hostage. The longer you talk and the longer you negotiate, the lower the anxiety level of the holder becomes. Police have offered food, drink, sex, money, and escape in hostage situations which have resulted in the surrender of the holder and release of the hostages. No demand is too bizarre to be accepted for consideration, even though the demand may be completely impossible to provide. Again, slow down! Don't rush a situation. Prepare for a long siege and take the necessary steps to tactically deal with the prolonged situation. The negotiation technique used in a suicide or barricade situation is similar. Concessions can be made on both sides with complete abandonment of the subject's suicidal plan as the final goal. Remember, most people want to be talked to and will welcome a problem-solving path out of their dilemma if it is put to them in a sympathetic, understanding approach.

THE ROLE OF THE NEGOTIATOR

As soon as some background information is received about the holder and the scene is tactically ready for continuous negotiations, an attempt should be made to communicate with the subject. As a negotiator, you should first introduce yourself and, if asked, admit that you are a police officer. Keep your rank to yourself. If you introduce yourself as a Chief of Police, you will not have available the ploy of checking with superiors on demands made by the holder. If the first contact is to be made by telephone or bullhorn, make sure that the holder gets the name of someone he can deal with. Do not get caught in an obvious lie, and do not make concessions that the holder will know you are not authorized to make. Do not make promises too readily. Advise him that you will have to talk it over with superiors, although he may demand that the superiors do the negotiation if you keep referring everything "up the ladder." You can, however, make minor concessions yourself. Make sure that you sound sincere. Many people, particularly those who are mentally disturbed, can read insincerity or outright lies into your tone of voice. Make concessions, but don't become a pawn. Don't let the holder lead you around. Don't give up everything. If face-to-face negotiation finally takes place, be careful about body language and facial expressions. This also can be read by a sensitive person as a signal that you are lying or that you are attempting to gain control of the situation by subterfuge and eventual violence. If he does not use profanity, do not use it yourself. Aim for the transference of thoughts between you and the holder. If you can finally "read" him, associate yourself with his problem and, if he believes you are sincerely attempting to help him, the situation will be much easier to handle.

Be careful about using relatives and friends. The main reason the man may be involved in his situation is possibly due to his wife. When she is brought to the scene, it may set him off and produce a violent end to the incident. The same holds true of members of the clergy, psychiatrists and psychologists, and other relatives. Make sure that you know what the subject's feeling is about those people before you allow them to get anywhere near him or even let him know that they are in the vicinity. Many holders will ask for a member of the press to act as an intermediary, but an attempt should be made to talk him out of this demand. There may be situations where he will only talk to the media; however, keep in mind that the goals of the media are usually altogether different from the aims of the police. Most police agencies will admit to unhappy experiences in dealing with hostage situations where the media are involved. If a law enforcement agency is forced into having an intermediary deal with the hostage, make sure that a member of the negotiating team can overhear all of the conversations and guide the intermediary along the accepted lines of negotiation. Other than in-person negotiation, the telephone is the next best method of communication. However, dealing with a person on the telephone is difficult, while effective negotiation by bullhorn is next to impossible. No holder can relate to a loudspeaker, and traditionally all that comes out of a police bullhorn is a threatening monologue. For the same reason, do not use a loud bullhorn for giving orders to officers at the scene while negotiations are being attempted or are in progress. Make sure that liaison is maintained with members of the precision firearms or SWAT teams. Keep in mind that a gun or any other weapon is nonnegotiable. If this stipulation is strongly made to any request by the holder at the outset, the police should be on better grounds. The police should never volunteer to take the place of the hostage. A police hostage results in emotional response by other police and could result in overreaction and the taking of unnecessary risks. A police hostage may also be in much greater danger than most other hostages. The holder has a built-in focal point for his frustrations when he holds a life and death power over a symbol of authority. Generally, a stranger being held as a hostage is in much less danger than a police officer, friend or relative, or other symbol of authority. The role of the negotiator during the period of time that he is effectively dealing with the subject in a crisis situation should be recognized by the agency as being of prime importance. He should be backed up by all the available resources of the department and should guide the tactical approach to the incident. His assessment of the subject should set the tone of the police activity at the scene. If an overt police presence is needed or a low-key approach is warranted, his recommendation should be accepted. He should not be expected to start face-to-face negotiation unless he feels comfortable and completely safe and only after some dialogue has taken place. In short, his is not a suicide mission.

Chapter TWO   FORMATION OF A
POLICE HOSTAGE NEGOTIATION TEAM

POLICY OF THE DEPARTMENT

AFTER the establishment of the Department Policy regarding negotiations, the formation and organization of a negotiating team should be considered. Assignments to the team should be a collateral duty, but when a hostage situation is in progress, this function should assume primary importance. It is necessary that the top management of the department announce its full accord with the concept of negotiating and indicate its complete support of the team to be organized.

CHOOSING THE CANDIDATE

The task of choosing the candidates for a negotiating team is difficult. First we should look for an all around "good cop"; someone with common sense, ability to get along with people, and a talent for coping with unpleasant situations. The candidate should have above-average intelligence and have some experience in interviewing and interrogation. Rank is relatively unimportant. The team should represent the community; that is, it should reflect the racial composition of the society it serves. It is recommended that one quarter to one third of the team should be females if they are available and meet the basic requirements. The age of the candidate is not important since the persons who are going to be dealt with will run the gamut from teenagers to the elderly. The educational background of the negotiators, although not considered to be of prime importance, can be looked upon as an aid in the overall training of the team. For example, those members with some prior exposure to the concepts of psychology can more readily understand some of the problems that the team may be facing and be able to deal with them in a more professional manner.

All candidates should be volunteers. The intention of the department to form a team should be announced and volunteers solicited. All prospective candidates should be asked to review the published policy of the department, and then interviews of each candidate should be conducted to determine mental attitude in regard to the concept of negotiation, as opposed to the traditional police response to a hostage situation. Candidates with ethnic hangups should be avoided. Thin-skinned and easily aggravated individuals will not be able to successfully perform in high crisis situations. These interviews should be conducted by the top or middle management of the police department, and if possible, a psychological consultant should be present. Further psychological testing of each candidate, prior to acceptance, should be considered. Tests for latent suicidal tendencies, underlying aggression, and general intelligence will be of value in eliminating those candidates whose personalities would be detrimental to negotiating. After the candidates are chosen, a general meeting should be held with all the individuals to be assigned to the team and the overall plan outlined. In some departments the candidates will know each other prior to formation of the team; however, in larger departments many will have little or no knowledge of the individuals they will be performing with. It is of vital importance that each negotiating team member eventually knows the capabilities and attitude for his or her peers. This will only come with training, particularly when role playing is used extensively. All questions pertaining to the department policies and procedures should be answered at the first general meeting, and a clear-cut support of the team should be generated. Suggestions and recommendations should be solicited from the candidates, and it should be explained that, when operational, the negotiating team will be a basically "rankless" organization.

TRAINING

If possible, the newly formed team should be trained by an agency that has had some hostage negotiating training and experience. If this is not practical, a self-training program can be instituted by using training outlines of other agencies and requesting some members of experienced agencies to at least lecture on their training and experience.*

Professional psychological or psychiatric assistance, if available, should be sought to assist in the training program. However, any professional psychologist/psychiatrist should completely understand the policy and goal of the department in this area before becoming involved in the training. Some agencies have established a training program and have been well into the psychological approach to a situation before realizing that the lecturer did not understand, or totally disagreed with, the concept of police negotiations. How well an outline can be molded into an effective training program really depends on the availability of experienced instructors. For future training it is vitally important that any operation or situation be critiqued with all available members present. Any situation occurring in surrounding jurisdictions should be reviewed by the unit as soon as practical after the incident and as soon as personnel who were involved can be persuaded to talk about their experiences. After the unit is selected, tested, and trained, a simple call-out procedure for off-duty response should be established. The entire department should know that the team is available, under what conditions it should be called, and how to get it when it is needed. The number of personnel to be assigned to the negotiating team is dependent upon the number of personnel in the department, how many personnel of the team would be available at any specific time for response, and how many can effectively be trained. Four to five negotiators at the scene is an ideal operating unit.

THE TEAM AT THE SCENE

When the first member of the negotiating team arrives at the scene, his first priority will be to find the officer who knows as much about what has happened as possible and gather as much information as he can about the subject. He should verify with his dispatcher that other negotiators are responding, who they are, and decide whether any further help is going to be required. He should immediately establish the negotiators as part of the opera-

---

*See Appendix II for sample training outline.

tions at the scene. He must make it known to the superior officer
at the scene that the negotiators are present and how they can be
identified. As other negotiators arrive, and if negotiations are not
already in progress, "Talker One" and "Talker Two" should be
selected. These will be the prime and back-up negotiators. All
negotiators at the scene who will be taking part in the operation
should be completely briefed on exactly what has happened, and
a written negotiation log should be started. Intelligence gathering regarding the subject should start immediately, and all information important to the negotiations should be relayed to
"Talker One" and "Talker Two" continuously during the incident. All equipment to back up negotiation effort should be
directed to the location where the negotiators are setting up.
Negotiators must verify that the officer in charge of the incident
is fully cognizant of their presence, plans, and procedures. The
negotiators have to identify the policies that this officer will be
following in regard to the media, assault teams, precision firearms
teams, escape of the individual, and anything else that would
interfere with a successful negotiation.

Part of the overall training effort should be simulated incidents where the tactics of the negotiators at the scene are instituted and practiced. As the experience of the team increases
through training or actual incidents, a more professional approach to an incident will be forthcoming. If other officers observe a well-organized group of their own agency coolly performing
their tasks despite the confusion of a crisis situation, an overall
calming effect can result. The spin-off benefit of the formation
of a negotiating team will be the recognition throughout the department that this technique is available as a possibility for
approaching a high anxiety situation with less than a "storm
trooper" attitude. Once the team is formed, organized, trained, and
has had some experience it should be used as a training resource
for the entire department, for many of the principles used in the
negotiations are very effective when included in crisis intervention training.

ROLE PLAYING

Many police officers think little of the training value of role playing. However, they are usually amazed at the utility of the role playing involved in a simulated hostage situation training program. Role playing before a crowd usually results in a stiff, awkward dramatization of an incident, but if there is nothing but a television camera and a technician in the room where the skit is taking place, the untrained actors react much more readily. The ideal technique for effective role playing is to have the actors in one room, the viewers in another, with closed circuit television linking the rooms. In the beginning, a negotiating team with little familiarity or knowledge of each other usually does not take readily to role playing as a training aid; however, once it begins it obviously becomes such an ideal method of training that even the shyest person becomes totally involved. There is no better way of bringing a hostage situation into a classroom than role playing. The audience can comment freely upon the mistakes being made by negotiator—actor, and the entire theory and tactics of negotiation and the techniques of dealing with high anxiety situations are brought home. Often, the participants in the real-life role playing incidents become so completely carried away that they must be curtailed. An excellent device is to salt the incident with a very uncooperative hostage who continuously interferes with the negotiations, so that the frustration level of the negotiator is raised. The personality, frustration level, ethnic slur tolerance, and aggressiveness of each negotiator who takes part in a few role playing incidents becomes known to all, and a judgment can then be made by team members as to who should be used at an actual, live incident. If possible, the role of the holder, the barricaded subject, or the suicide should be played by some-one other than a team member and, better still, someone who is not known at all to the negotiating team.

CRITIQUES

The critique of an actual incident is probably one of the best training methods other than actual role playing. All team members may not be at every incident, so that a detailed review of the actions taken by a few of the negotiators is an invaluable aid to the other team members. A review of the procedures that worked, those that did not, the tactics used, and the thoughts and reactions of the negotiators who were involved is very useful. Attempts should be made to attend critiques conducted by other departments of incidents in their own areas. A free flow of this type of information back and forth between negotiating teams results in a high level library of knowledge of what technique to use and what not to use. Every incident is different, but the basic concepts remain the same. We have to react to the individuals involved, but our reactions should follow along similar guidelines so that a firm procedure can be followed until experience dictates that it has to change. Taped recordings made during an actual incident are of great value during a critique of the incident. Also, any photographs, television tapes, or movies of the incident taken by the media should be borrowed and examined after the incident. This type of hindsight usually leads to not only change and improvement in the methods of the negotiating team, but also improvement in the tactics, policies, and procedures of the entire agency.

Chapter Three   TACTICAL
APPROACH TO A HOSTAGE SITUATION

FAMILIARIZATION WITH POLICY

IF A NEGOTIATING team is to effectively deal with a high anxiety situation and expects to accomplish its prime objective—the release of the hostage, the surrender of the barricaded person, or the dissuasion of the person attempting suicide—there must be some tactical plan. The disseminated department policy should outline a basic plan for these situations. Experience has shown that it is much easier for a negotiating team to operate effectively if they are part of an overall organizational framework that is proceeding along accepted guidelines. If police tactics at the scene lack discipline and result in confusion, the negotiating team may have great difficulty in dealing with a subject who is able to perceive the degree of chaos with which the police are operating. Lack of a tactical plan is not only a hinderance, but an absolute danger to the operating negotiating team. There should never be any doubt as to who is in charge at the scene. That officer must "have a handle" on the whole operation. He has to know what the negotiating team is attempting to accomplish and must be informed of any important change of tactics as the negotiations progress. This person, whether a Sergeant or a Chief, has to be completely familiar with the overall department policy governing police activities at the scene.

FIRST OFFICER AT THE SCENE

To the negotiator, the interview with the first officer at the scene is of great importance. However, sometimes the officer who knows most about what has happened may be unwittingly sent to another area, frustrating the debriefing process. He may even have had some conversation with the holder or hostage, be familiar with the interior of the building, or have some prior knowledge of the parties involved that may aid in negotiations. Despite all this knowledge available to aid in dealing with the situation, he may be the first officer designated to go for coffee. The negotiating team then has to seek out this officer and find out exactly what he knows. As established by department procedure, the first officer's job when he arrives at the scene of a possible hostage/barricade/suicide attempt situation is to obtain as much information as possible and report that information by radio, telephone, or in person to someone who can evaluate it. The first officer should attempt to contain and isolate the situation. As further help arrives, the necessary evacuation should take place, and both vehicle and pedestrian traffic should be rerouted. A line of communication must be established, whether by phone to a neighboring home or by radio to a designated patrol car. Firearms discipline should be strictly enforced. No shots should be fired unless a life is at stake. If shots are or have been fired, the necessary standby medical help should be requested. In-depth negotiations should be avoided at this time, but if communications have started with the holder, they should be allowed to continue.

SUPERIOR OFFICER

When the first patrol supervisor or other superior officer arrives at the scene, he should take command of the situation, announce that he is in command, and let it be known how he can be reached. A secure command post should be established along with a safe staging area for other responding units. An inner and outer perimeter of the operation should be designated. The outer perimeter should be the line where all traffic stops and no unauthorized persons are allowed access. The primary command post should be on the edge of the outer perimeter, and supervising officers of the various commands responding to the situation should report to the officer in charge at that command post.* The command post must be in a safe area but convenient to the center of operations. If practical, all residents should be evacuated from inside the outer perimeter. The inner perimeter, that is the line

---

*See Appendix III for perimeter diagrams.

which no one but the precision firearms/assault teams and hostage negotiators can cross, should be established. All uniformed personnel can then be evacuated from inside the inner perimeter and take up designated positions between perimeters or on the line of the outer perimeter. Again, firearms discipline should be strictly enforced, and communications between the negotiators and precision firearms/assault teams and all officers inside the perimeters should be firmly maintained. A media liaison officer should be designated, and all questions regarding the situation proposed to the agency by the media must be directed to him. All media representatives arriving at the scene can be directed to report to him near the outer perimeter command post. Any representative of the media inside the outer perimeter should be removed if he does not confine himself to the media reception area. Photographs of the entire operation are of value and should be taken by the agency. All conversations between the subject and the negotiator should be recorded at the command post, and a written log must be maintained of all important points of the negotiations. A separate command post log can be maintained in the command post under the direction of the superior officer in charge.

POLICE ACTIVITY

Obvious police activity in view of the holder or subject of the situation should be kept to a minimum. There is nothing more disconcerting to an emotionally disturbed person than police moving back and forth armed with shotguns and wearing bullet-proof vests and riot helmets. When negotiators are attempting to calm this person the background activity that may be in his view negates the calming effect of the negotiator. The communications should be emphasized as being of prime importance. However, the use of loudspeakers and noisy police radios should be kept to a minimum so that the overall atmosphere does not appear threatening to the subject. To avoid general confusion over police communications, the use of numerical or alphabetical designations of posts, areas, or buildings should be avoided. Plain language should be used, and the use of "10 codes" or other codes not established specifically by the officer in charge of the situation should be avoided. Police officers on duty in outlying traffic areas must be informed of the basic problems and kept informed of all stages of the situation in case an egress that will penetrate the inner and outer perimeters is imminent. The necessary equipment at the scene will naturally depend on the weapon being used by the subject. If the subject is armed with a knife, the equipment needed to combat the situation will be different than if he is armed with a rifle or a shotgun. If he claims to possess explosives or a bomb, naturally the necessary equipment to handle that situation has to be available. The establishment of inner and outer perimeters, how large they should be, and how much evacuation should take place also depends on the weapon involved. For example, the inner and outer perimeter size, the area covered, and the level of evacuation would be minimal if the subject was armed with a knife.

COMMAND POST FUNCTIONS

The command post, in addition to overseeing the entire operations, should also maintain a liaison with any utility company that may be required to respond to the scene: telephone, lighting, air conditioning, heating, water, fire department, etc. A list of phone numbers of these agencies and the name of the person to call when immediate response is necessary should be established. If there is a possibility that a nonlethal weapon, such as tear gas of the burning type, is to be used, the fire department should be notified and must respond to the scene in a standby status. All decisions that would affect the life of a hostage or the holder must be made at the command post. No independent action may be taken by the precision firearms or assault teams without that direction. It is up to the command post to advise everyone when an authorized shot is to be fired, and this only after consultation with negotiators, if negotiations are in progress.

DEALING WITH THE MEDIA

There have been cases in the New York City metropolitan area in which the holder of hostages, due to live television and/or radio broadcasts, knew more about the police operation than most of the police officers involved. Live television coverage of a scene can negate effective negotiations when the police negotiators are attempting to play down the situation and television depicts the activity of police preparing for a siege. Attempts at interviewing the holder or the hostages, by telephone and in person, have been made by representatives of the media while the situations were in progress. A police agency should be prepared to deal with the media and elicit their cooperation by designating a media liaison officer. This officer should feed reporters as much information as possible without interfering with negotiations. However, no live interviews of police personnel should be conducted while negotiations are in progress unless the negotiators themselves have briefed the individual to be interviewed. There have been situations where the negotiators have spent hours convincing the holder to follow one line of thinking, and then he hears a contradicting statement given by another officer during a television interview. It is a highly dangerous practice to allow this type of interview during the course of operations at a hostage situation.

No entry of the outer perimeter should be made by any representatives of the media with or without escort, except to the designated area set aside for the media. If the holder is in his own home and his phone number is listed, his name should not be given to the media, so that there are no interfering telephone calls. If the situation is taking place in a commercial building such as a bank, with more than one telephone number, it will be difficult for the police to control media attempts to interview one or more of the subjects involved. However, if a designated media liaison officer is appointed, he can attempt to impress the representatives of the media at the scene with the need for cooperation.

PREPARATION FOR A MOVE

During the incident the law enforcement agency could be forced into allowing a move by the holder and hostages, and the necessary preparation should be considered. If the holder demands a vehicle of a specific type, a miniature bugging device should be available for immediate installation. Appropriate direction-finding equipment, if available, should be attached and follow-up cars designated and equipped with tracking receivers. If possible, a remote ignition-control device should be installed on the vehicle to be used by the holder and hostages.* If the probable route or destination is known, officers in these areas should be contacted and be told exactly what tactics are to be followed. If the destination is outside the jurisdictional boundary of the agency involved at the scene, immediate liaison with the adjoining agency should be established and maintained. Policy decisions involving interagency operation must be established prior to a hostage situation and not when a car full of hostages is en route. If, for example, the hostages are being moved from one jurisdiction to an airport in another agency's area of responsibility, the policy governing airport property should be followed as soon as the incident is moved into that realm of responsibility. Various governmental agencies should meet and make their respective policies known to each other in the event a hostage situation develops which crosses political or jurisdictional boundary lines.

PREPARATION FOR AN EXTENDED SESSION

As the situation progresses, the police must immediately start to prepare for the worst, that is, a long-term incident. The agency should adopt an on-the-scene "think tank" concept, not a headquarters-control operation. For example, if an evacuation of people inside the inner and outer perimeters has taken place, facilities for the comfort of these evacuated citizens should be provided for in schools, firehouses, or other public buildings. Various other problems associated with the evacuation and isolation of an area for a prolonged period of time will have to be overcome by the police, as public acceptance will be dependent upon the resourcefulness of the agency in handling these problems. Naturally, the comfort of the officers involved over a prolonged period should also be considered. Frequent relief, availability of food and drink, sanitary facilities, and ability to contact home should be considered if the agency is going to run a success-

---

*See Appendix IV for description of electronic equipment.

ful operation. There are still other problems usually associated with long-term incidents that have to be considered. Emergency lighting will no doubt be needed during some phase of a prolonged session. Emergency generators usually arrive on the scene with full gasoline tanks; however, some agencies have limited facilities for providing refueling of emergency equipment at the scene of an incident. In addition, it will not take long, particularly if the radio traffic is heavy, for walkie-talkie batteries to weaken. A supply of spare batteries, or the means for recharging the units, should be brought to the scene to maintain effective communications. The command post should monitor local weather forecasts so that changes in the weather that will affect the operation can be prepared for. Long-range planning is of prime importance; for example, if the incident takes place on a weekend and there is a school nearby, plans for handling an influx of children into the near vicinity should be made. The effect on police patrol, while the situation is in progress and immediately after the incident is closed, has to be considered. A large-scale incident usually exhausts police resources in a small or medium-sized agency, and the effect of a serious cutback in patrol upon the community has to be considered.

Chapter Four   EQUIPPING
A NEGOTIATING TEAM

M UCH of the basic equipment that could be required at the scene of an incident may already be available in most departments. One of the main objects of a negotiating team should be a survey of the equipment believed to be needed, where it is located, and how to get it in a hurry. If some items considered to be important to the operation are not in the inventory of the agency, steps should be taken to purchase or manufacture the items. In any case, the negotiating team should train with whatever equipment is available. In some agencies it may be possible for the negotiating team to be thoroughly familiar with all of the equipment, but in other larger departments, it may be more practical for specialized back-up units that are thoroughly familiar with sophisticated electronic equipment to respond to the scene to assist the negotiators. These specialists should be included in the call-out procedure and take part in the training program of the negotiating team. Basically, the team must know what is available, where it is, how to get it, and how to use it when it gets there. If specialists respond, they should be completely "tuned" to the mission of the negotiators through joint training sessions.

BASIC EQUIPMENT

One of the most important pieces of equipment that the department can supply the team is bullet-proof vests, of the type that can be worn under the shirt. If there are female members on the team, suitable vests must be provided for them. The negotiators should also be provided with some type of identifiable outerwear, such as a light nylon jacket with suitable identifying insignia or lettering on the back. In many cases, negotiators will be responding in civilian clothes, and since they will be allowed into the inner perimeter of the operation, all members of the department have to be aware of who they are. The negotiation team kit may also provide for protective clothing such as coveralls and head gear for operation in unusual areas and conditions.

ENTRY EQUIPMENT

Forcible entry equipment such as crowbars, Halligan tools, Detroit door openers, pinch bars, and hammers and nails should be provided in the assault team or the negotiating team kit. This kit should also contain a tape measure of at least 100 feet in length so that measurements outside a building can pinpoint inside areas. Along with forcible entry tools, rope and wedges, which can be used to prevent the surprise use of a door by an armed subject, are a valuable addition to the kit. The quiet and efficient use of forcible entry and surprise exit equipment should be included in the overall training program.

POLICE EQUIPMENT

Normal police equipment such as binoculars, flashlights, bullhorns, telephone directories, street maps of the local area, and large-scale maps of the surrounding area, utility company telephone numbers, liquid tear gas, and so on can also be part of the kit. A first aid kit, fire extinguisher, and standard department walkie-talkies should also be available. The potential use of all of this standard equipment in a hostage situation is rather obvious; additional equipment can be added as the specific need is uncovered.

SPECIAL POLICE EQUIPMENT

Experience has shown that some special items, if available, can be of great value at the scene of a hostage situation. A night vision device, periscope, bomb blankets, and dog repellant have all shown their value in various types of incidents. A listing of telephone numbers of various officials of government agencies in the area should also be considered for inclusion as special equipment. Photographic equipment may be added to the kit as means will allow. Hideaway weapons can be provided in accordance with the agency policy as to whether the negotiating team is to be involved in the neutralization of the subject.

ELECTRONIC EQUIPMENT

A telephone amplifier — a simple device in which a cup fitted over the earpiece of a phone enables all persons in the room to hear the other end of the conversation — is extremely valuable during a telephone negotiation session. Another useful tool is the small wireless microphone or miniature transmitter to be worn by "Talker One," the prime negotiator, with a companion receiver at the command post where all conversations will be recorded. "Talker Two," the secondary negotiator, should have a small pocket receiver on the same frequency, with an earpiece, so he can hear all the conversation in which "Talker One" is involved. "Talker Two" should have available as a back-up, a walkie-talkie for communication with the command post. The necessary wiretap and eavesdrop bugging equipment should also be provided. A telephone instrument with at least 100 feet of cable terminating in alligator clips could also be provided for interruption of the service in the building involved. A supply of recording tape and batteries for all electronic equipment must be provided in the kit. Direction-tracking equipment, or what is generally known as a "bumper beeper," if available, should be dispatched to the scene of any hostage situation. Naturally, all wiretap/eavesdrop activities should be undertaken under the constraints of local and federal law. It should be noted that federal law does not permit police emergency wiretapping or bugging without court order.

VEHICLES

If the department is able to supply the hostage negotiation team with a vehicle, much of the above-listed equipment can be housed in a suitable container and kept in the trunk. If possible, this vehicle should be the car that will be turned over to the holder if his demand for transportation away from the scene is to be granted. For this purpose, special equipment may be installed to overhear any conversation in the vehicle and also to remotely control the ignition system of the car.* If a vehicle is equipped such as this, it must be considered a limited-use vehicle in the department.

MISCELLANEOUS

At the scene of any hostage situation, an ambulance, gas masks, oxygen, and tools should be available. Of course, the necessary trained personnel to operate all of this equipment will be contacted and ordered to report to the scene. Naturally, if there is a bomb involved, Bomb Squad or Explosive Ordnance Disposal personnel should be standing by. If the agency is fortunate in having a command-post vehicle, its value at the scene of a hostage situation is obvious. Much of the equipment mentioned, particularly the directional tracking, "bumper beeper" transmitters, is battery operated and sensitive to temperature changes. Battery life should be tested in both ends of the temperature variation normally attributed to the area of operation.

If it is to be the policy of the department that the negotiating team should be involved in any attempt to neutralize the holder, the necessary small weapons should be provided. The small .25 caliber automatic is virtually useless, whereas the .22 magnum, or larger caliber, two-shot derringer is effective at close range. A hideaway gun in a hostage/negotiating team car is not recommended unless a unique hiding place that is easily accessible is provided. Naturally, if it is decided that the negotiating team should take part in the neutralization of the holder, firearms training with any special weapons must be provided.

AT THE SCENE

Upon arrival at the scene of the situation, the negotiating team should first suit up, that is, put on the bullet-proof vests and identifiable outerwear. While part of the team is obtaining the necessary intelligence, the remainder should be assessing what equipment is at the scene and begin getting it ready for use. If they have the luxury of specialist back-up they should be instruc-

---

*See Appendix IV for description of vehicle equipment.

ting the back-up unit as to the type of equipment which will probably be put into use. All the equipment should be checked and
its capability for immediate use should be verified. "Talker
One," that is, the prime negotiator, should be equipped with his
wireless microphone. "Talker Two" should be equipped with a
small receiver on the same frequency as the wireless microphone,
plus a walkie-talkie set at the channel of operation of the incident.
Even if negotiation is to start by telephone or bullhorn, these
team members should be equipped and ready in case the situation
changes rapidly. Necessary receiving and recording equipment
should be set up and ready for operation in the command post.
The team vehicle, if it is specially equipped, must have all the
equipment removed from it and put into position of readiness
for the possibility of turning it over to the holder. A negotiation
log should be established so that all of the conversations with the
holder can be listed and important points identified that may be
of value for subsequent negotiations. The building in which the
holder is confined should be inspected surreptitiously and a
sketch drawn that will show points of entry and exit and other
areas where utilities such as heat and electric, telephone, television cable, etc. can be interrupted. If the premises are a commercial building such as a bank, the main telephone panel, if outside the area of the holder, should be located and telephone company personnel requested at the scene. The response of utility
company personnel should also be considered in case electricity,
water, air conditioning, etc. are to be interrupted. The agency's
photographic unit should be present at the scene and start photo-
graphing as soon as they arrive. Photographs are invaluable at
later court presentations and also serve to aid the negotiators in
future critiques and training sessions.

It costs little to outfit a team, and many departments will find
that most of the needed equipment is already on board. If any
additional items are considered necessary, they probably will be
of the type of equipment that can be used for many other law
enforcement purposes in addition to the once-in-awhile negotiating team use.

Chapter Five   DEALING
WITH THE SUBJECT

"STREET PSYCHOLOGY"

THE TRAINING of a police agency in the art of negotiation, whether it be the in-depth training of a team of hostage negotiators or a department-wide program in crisis intervention, can be of immense value to the agency. The day to day activities of the police agency bring the police officer face to face with family disturbances, neighborhood feuds, suicide attempts, emotionally disturbed persons in various situations, and, finally, actual barricade and/or hostage incidents. There is really no great mystery attached to the successful handling of each of the situations. However, the importance of adhering to the overall department policy increases as the situations become more critical and the danger to life increases. The role of the police officer in each case is that of a negotiator; that is, he is trying to trade off something to get some type of concession from the person he is dealing with. Most of the dangerous stiuations, that is, those involving emotionally disturbed persons, are highly fluid, and the experienced police officer should be ready to alter his method of approach in midstream.

The prime objective is, naturally, to protect life, whether it be that of a hostage, of the barricaded person, or of the mentally disturbed person attempting suicide. The officer has to rely on what I like to call "street psychology:" that is, the common sense that he started with as a police officer, plus his knowledge and capability of handling people, gained during whatever period of time he has spent as an active law enforcement officer. He has to be careful about what to say and what not to say. His body language and facial expression should not contradict what he is mouthing. He has to try to identify the type of person he is dealing with. If he can identify the frustration, conflict, and anxiety

35

of the subject and extract from him the reasons that these conditions exist, he can then attempt to aid the subject in problem solving. He should remember that excessive anxiety tends to make a person extremely sensitive and sharpens the senses. The police officer should attempt to decrease anxiety and not add to it. He should be calm, he should listen, and he should exhibit a genuine interest in the problems of the person he is dealing with.

He should not attempt to convey to the person that he is the answer to all the problems, but he should assist in developing a problem-solving atmosphere, thereby reducing the awareness and anxiety of the subject. Time is the most effective ally to the negotiator. There is an automatic decrease in anxiety with the passage of time. A time limit should never be put on the actions of the subject. Some incidents have been successfully concluded after having lasted for days. There are many things that help reduce anxiety: sleep, sex, comfort, and a feeling of safety can aid in preventing the high anxiety "full cup" of emotions from overflowing during negotiations with any individual. In face-to-face negotiations, the police officer-negotiator should be careful about intruding upon the intimate space of the subject. Depending upon his emotional condition, this intimate space could extend from an area that the subject can touch without moving, to the full interior of a room. If the officer can read the intimate space established in the mind of the person, he should then be careful in all future movements from intruding upon it. The intrusion of a stranger upon an emotionally disturbed person's space can be detrimental to effectively dealing with the person.

Another situation that may surface is the degree of acceptance of the physical appearance of a negotiator to the subject. A uniformed police officer may "turn off" the subject being dealt with. If this happens, he must be immediately replaced by a plainclothes officer. Also, if the subject is a conservative middle-aged man, the typical college-boy appearance of the negotiator may not result in effective transference. If possible, try to match the subject with the negotiator.

In summary, don't be a "patsy" and agree with everything; offer alternatives to the course being set by the subject; let him know you want to listen and help; be sincere and mean it; let him talk so you can identify his problems; offer him realistic alternatives to solving his problems; negotiate, don't be a pawn. If there is a hostage involved, try to get some concessions for everything you give.

During the training of a group in the art of dealing with a subject, the use of a bullhorn, a telephone, and a radio should be practiced. Many persons find it easy to deal with another while face to face; however, when the parties are separated and the telephone is in use, it becomes extremely difficult. One cannot read the body language or the facial expressions of another, and there is difficulty interpreting voice tones and inflections. The effectiveness of a bullhorn in negotiating is almost nonexistent. The mechanical squawk of a bullhorn can be extremely threatening to an emotionally disturbed person, particularly if associated with armed police officers in the vicinity. There have been cases where the person barricaded without a telephone available has been convinced to accept a walkie-talkie and converse with the police by use of the radio. Naturally, this is no more effective than a telephone; in fact, it is somewhat less effective due to the necessity of the mechanical operation of an unfamiliar piece of equipment by the subject.

Police should train in the use of these items and be aware of the effectiveness or noneffectiveness of each piece of equipment. Naturally, if a telephone is in use, all conversations should be recorded or at least amplified so that more than one negotiator can overhear the other end of the conversation. The use of an intermediary is not recommended; however, it is sometimes a necessity, particularly when there is a language barrier. Be careful when an interpreter is being used unless the interpreter is another police officer. An interpreter who is a friend or neighbor of the subject may not relate to the negotiator all of the conversations necessary for him to make a judgment of the intentions of the subject. The goal of transference cannot really be attained through an interpreter. Friends, neighbors, family, clergy, etc. also come under suspicion, and considerable evaluation should be made before they are allowed to deal with the subject. Only after in-depth intelligence is gathered should any one of these persons be allowed within the sight of the subject.

Even without a formal hostage negotiating team within the agency, the training should instill within officers the idea that negotiations are a team effort. For example, the first officer negotiating with the subject may "run dry." In other words, he may run out of things to say that will keep the attention of the subject. It is now time for him to introduce his replacement. The art of exiting the situation and introducing a replacement that will be accepted by the subject should be practiced. This can usually be accomplished by introducing the replacement as one step up in rank from the original negotiator. This is one of the reasons why the negotiator, if in plain clothes, should always introduce himself as a police officer, even if he is a superior officer.

DEALING WITH THE HOSTAGE

In many cases the hostage can become an adversary of the negotiator without the negotiator realizing it. Psychologists indicate that, in a prolonged hostage situation, a group relationship develops; that is, the hostage and the holder may actually become friendly. The hostage tends to believe that he or she owes the holder something for not killing him, or a quasi-friendship develops whereby the hostage may, in fact, aid the holder by telling him of police activities. In no case should the hostage be completely trusted. In many cases the hostage can interfere and be a hindrance to negotiations, especially in family situations. Officers should be trained to avoid prolonged conversations with the hostage and reserve their attention completely for the holder. There is a possibility that a hostage may have to be admonished if he or she interferes with negotiations, and this could result in reinforcing the holder as to his being the center of attraction and in lessening the importance of the hostage to the holder.

In some family cases, the negotiator may, in fact, have sympathy with the holder. This often happens when the holder, although he has taken some drastic action and may be a threat to everyone concerned, has a hostage-wife who obviously is the cause of his problem. The first course of action on the part of the negotiator in this situation is to get the hostage quiet and to continue to deal sympathetically with the husband. However, the reverse can often happen. The holder can exhibit such an abrasive personality and continue to insult the negotiator, police, and society in general, that the negotiator may rapidly build up an actual hatred for the subject. This resentment of the subject on the part of the negotiator cannot be obvious to the subject if effective negotiations are to take place.

DEALING WITH THE USE OF DRUGS

If it can be determined that the holder is under the influence of drugs or alcohol, it is of extreme importance to determine the type he has taken. For example, the negotiator may think it is all right to allow liquor to be used as a trade-off during negotiations in order to calm the holder. However, there are certain drugs that may produce a temporary violent reaction if there is the addition of liquor into the body.

A holder on amphetamine or "ups" will gradually become calmer if he is isolated from his supply, and usually the incident will "wind down." A subject on barbituates or "downs" may start getting excited unless the negotiator can perceive his conditions and introduce a supply.

Naturally, any activity of this type should only be taken with the advice of a physician who is thoroughly briefed on the statements and actions of the subject and can identify the particular drug taken.

Be careful of a "garbage head," who is on anything he can get and may be mixing ups, downs, and who-knows-what else, or the person on hallucinogenics, who is also unpredictable.

Some suggest that, during a hostage situation, if the holder asks for food or drink, the police should attempt to introduce "knock-out drops" or a sleep-inducing drug into the item to be consumed. This is worth considering and it has worked; however, if the holder becomes suspicious and forces a hostage to try the food or drink first, one could have a real problem. Again, if this tactic is to be attempted, medical aid should be available to treat whoever is effected by the drug, and a doctor should be involved in determining the type and quantity of the drug involved.

CHOOSING "TALKER ONE"

When the initial intelligence is gathered after arrival at the scene, the negotiators have to decide on the prime negotiator. For example, if the subject to be dealt with is a young male, an attempt should be made initially to match his age bracket. However, in many cases a more mature-appearing negotiator may actually relate better to the subject if a "father figure" of authority is doing the talking. If the negotiations have progressed to a face-to-face situation, a young negotiator can be tried, and if he does not "reach" the subject, he should be ready to use the ploy of introducing his boss and bowing out.

In dealing with a black subject, a black negotiator could be used; however, if he is being continually categorized as an "Uncle Tom" by the subject, his replacement by a white should be considered. Female negotiators can be used effectively if the background information indicates that no wife or girlfriend problems contributed to the subject's frame of mind.

In all cases "Talker One" should be ready to replace him– or herself if it is obvious that negotiations are at a standstill because of nonacceptance by the holder.

TRANSFERENCE

Transference is an automatic relationship between people as a result of an exchange of thoughts and ideas. It is important in negotiating to achieve as much possible insight into the person with whom one is dealing. Continued conversation about himself, things he likes and dislikes, future plans, problems, and alternative methods of dealing with his problems should be encouraged. Eventually, a feeling of transference may develop, and the negotiator can then guide the individual into a more peaceful problem-solving train of thought. A word of caution: be careful of becoming complacent in dealing with emotionally disturbed persons. It is possible for a negotiator to believe he has the subject convinced of his sincerity and interest and that the person is just about ready to capitulate when, in fact, the reverse can be true, and the subject may be just temporarily acquiescent. In other words, it may just be the lull before the storm, and the sought-after transference may never actually have been achieved.

In some cases, particularly in dealing with a criminal who has been around for a while, a too-sympathetic attitude on the part of the negotiator will come across as phony. He will believe that a cop is acting out of character and attempting to "con" him. The right mixture of firmness and willingness to make concessions, together with offering simple alternatives to the situation depending on the attitude of the subject, has to be exhibited. The best negotiator is the officer who can relate, in a believable manner, to the various characters and personalities with whom he is called upon to deal. If he can adapt his personality to the circumstances and attitude of the subject without showing his true feelings, he is well on the way to a successful conclusion to the situation.

There are no ironclad rules for dealing with people. Common sense and flexibility are the name of the game. Someday someone may write a book about how to deal with people in crisis that will answer all the questions about what to say and what not to say. A list of "trigger" words and actions to avoid would also be handy. As the study of human behavior continues, someone may eventually be able to tell us what type of emotional problem a person has after a few minutes of observation and then how to deal with it. Until then, we must use "street psychology" and our training and experience to cope with the problems of the people we serve.

CREDIBILITY

Some people were critical of the police in Indianapolis for not living up to their part of the bargain not to prosecute a hostage holder after release of the hostage in a recent incident.

On the other hand, many people, possibly even the same persons, criticized the Washington D.C. Police for allowing the leader of the Hanafi Muslims to go free without bond. Basically, the police are in a "damned if you do and damned if you don't" situation. I think the circumstances involved in each case should dictate what is and is not promised, after the threat to human life is evaluated. After it is over, the decision has to be made about how many of the promises should be kept.

Really, the less said about cases like these in the media, the better. Prospective hostage holders should not be assured that the same outcome will result every time a hostage is taken. The credibility of the negotiator is important; however, the public should be assured that hostages cannot be taken at will without eventual punishment of the holder.

Chapter Six TRAINING

THE LEARNING PROCESS OF NEGOTIATION

THE INTRODUCTORY training of a negotiator should probably start with an instruction session something akin to that outlined in Appendix II. The formal lectures on theory and tactics are important, the "Dos" and "Don'ts" of negotiation are necessary, and the role playing sessions are good practice. But the best teacher, as usual, is experience. Naturally, all members of an agency cannot participate in all phases of every actual negotiation incident, so there must be a critique, preferably attended by all involved.

Some "not so obvious at the time" facts become apparent during the critique sessions: Emotionally disturbed people are usually highly perceptive. This was pointed out in one recent early Sunday morning incident. A young man had barricaded himself in his apartment with a loaded .30 caliber carbine and threatened suicide if anyone attempted to enter the room where he had confined himself. Negotiations had progressed to a semi-face-to-face condition. The subject noticed that one of the negotiators was dressed in a warm-up jacket and a baseball cap. He asked the negotiator if his actions were preventing the officer from attending a Sunday morning baseball game. The negotiator answered truthfully, "as a matter of fact you are." This statement seemed to irritate the subject and apparently implied a subdued time limit to the incident. Luckily, the second negotiator came into the conversation and stated that he had no place to go and would talk to the man as long as he felt like talking. The subject diverted his attention to the second negotiator, and, as it worked out, he eventually surrendered to negotiator number two. It was obvious that the prime negotiator had turned off the subject by allowing him to think that the negotiator's baseball game was more important than the highly volatile incident that the subject was involved in. This was not fully realized until the tape made during the incident was played back to the negotiating team during the critique of the incident.

Some alleged hostage situations, which prove to be unfounded, can result in at least some practice in tactical procedures, if nothing else. Recently, a twenty-eight-year-old male had an argument with his neighbor regarding whose right it was to park in front of his house. A shouting match ensued resulting in the subject running into his house and appearing on the sidewalk with a 12-gauge shotgun. The neighbors scattered, and the police were called to the scene. As officers arrived and confronted the man, he dropped the shotgun, ran into his house, and locked the doors. Information was gathered that indicated that his wife was home and that another shotgun was available in the house. Attempts by police to enter the house and to make verbal contact with the subject were in vain. The area was cordoned off, evacuation of the adjoining homes took place, traffic was stopped, and the negotiators were called to the scene. Communication was attempted unsuccessfully by telephone, and a loudspeaker was then used which did nothing but wake up the entire neighborhood. These attempts at communication with the subject lasted approximately two hours. Finally, it was decided to attempt to move closer and actually try an entry into the house while continuing to attempt to communicate. A door was opened, and negotiators entered the living room continually trying to contact the subject. Finally, after officers had crept to a position where the bedroom could be observed, it was obvious that both the subject and his wife were sleeping in bed. After the subject had been arrested and was en route to the psychiatric ward, he was asked why he did not respond to the communication efforts of the officers and why he kept many police officers with numerous pieces of equipment at bay resulting in his whole neighborhood being kept awake. His only response was, "I didn't hear you."

Coordination between the hostage negotiating team, the commanding officer of the incident, and the assault teams is recognized as being absolutely necessary to successfully conclude an incident. For example, police were called at noontime on a weekday to an apartment complex close to a commercial area that was crowded with traffic and shoppers. A woman had reported that a man with a shotgun had taken hostages and was holding them in one of the apartments. She stated that she had been threatened with the shotgun and that the subject had barricaded himself in her apartment with other female tenants of the building. A major police operation was instituted. Evacuation of the apartment complex and rerouting of traffic were ordered. Heavily armed police officers took up positions surrounding the apartment. Precision firearms teams moved into rooftop locations. Some fifteen members of the media and both newspaper and television cameramen arrived on the scene. Some well-meaning superior officers, believing that tear gas was going to be used, notified the Fire Department. It being lunch time, employees, jurors, and spectators from a nearby court complex arrived at the scene along with numerous shoppers and neighbors. Two police helicopters orbited the apartment complex. While all of this was going on, the crowd was swelling, confusion mounting, and while television and newspapers recorded it for posterity, the hostage negotiating team was interviewing the woman who started it all. She stated that various persons in a room with shotguns had been trying to get to her within the past week. She also stated that these persons had sent up mechanical bugs and insects, particularly mechanical bees that were programmed to "eat her up." She also alluded to the fact that two days before she had had an argument with her neighbor because of the noise coming from the neighbor's vacuum cleaner. This confrontation was confirmed by the neighbor, whose colorful opinion of the woman's mental state left little room for doubt. It did not take long for the negotiators to realize that they had a completely irrational person on their hands and that nothing she said made any sense whatsoever. The key to her apartment was secured and entry made; however, because of a breakdown in communications, police reinforcements continued to arrive, the Fire Department prepared to put out a tear gas-started fire, the crowd enlarged, helicopters orbited, and the cameras continued to record the scene. The woman was hustled off to the psychiatric ward as the frustrated negotiating

team attempted to convince superior officers at the scene that all
the police activity was unnecessary. An incident such as this
readily points out the need for tactical improvement and can
actually be good for a department if the shortcomings are recognized. A later critique of the incident resulted in policy and
procedural changes that caused subsequent, more dangerous incidents to be handled in a more professional, efficient manner.

Negotiators have to be ready for anything. In another incident they were called to the scene to deal with an individual who
had allegedly assaulted his girlfriend and dragged her into a
condemned building where he lived, all the time waving a shotgun at passersby. Efforts by the police to communicate with the
individual were not successful. Negotiators arrived at the
cordoned-off scene and attempted to initiate communication by
bullhorn, as there was no telephone in the building. This was
not successful, and, after some tactical soul searching, it was decided to attempt a surreptitious entry into an area of the building
opposite the living quarters of the subject. Police officers on the
bedroom side of the building staged a diversion while negotiators
steathily entered through a boarded-up bathroom window. After
some difficulty in the darkened bathroom (one negotiator placed
his foot in a filled toilet bowl), the team proceeded into a darkened hallway to where they thought the bedroom door was
located. Much to their discomfort, they met an 80-pound German
shepherd in the middle of the dark hallway who indicated his dis-
pleasure at their intrusion by softly growling. They stated later
that this soft growling in the dark was much more frightening
than if he had barked. Both negotiators were armed with liquid
tear gas, and, although they were told that it probably would not
work on a dog, it was tried while they beat a hasty retreat into the
bathroom. The only effect the propelled tear gas had on the dog
was to make his soft growls a little louder. Eventually, this subject was apprehended in the bedroom, his girlfriend released (although she probably did not know she was a hostage), and the
shotgun recovered. The lesson learned from this incident by the
two negotiators in the darkened hallway is obvious. At the subsequent critique they indicated that "Talker One," after stepping

into a toilet and then meeting the dog in the dark, was probably no longer the best choice for negotiation with an armed subject, and that "Talker Two" was probably not much better. Dog repellent is now part of the equipment inventory.

It would be great if this or any other manual could be consulted at the scene of an incident and could give foolproof guidelines as to how to deal with each particular type of emotionally disturbed person, but such is not possible. For example, not long ago a young man casually walked through the front door of a local bank armed with a 12-gauge shotgun. He announced to the employees that he was there to get a date with one of the tellers and if he didn't, he would kill himself. Robbery alarm buttons were pressed while the subject walked over to one teller and engaged her in a conversation. The frightened girl, who did not know the subject, didn't know what to say. He continued to talk about going out on a date and kept threatening to shoot himself, until the first police officer arrived. The police officer, seeing a man with a shotgun in the center of a bank with customers and employees being held at bay, drew his own weapon and ordered the man to lower the shotgun. The subject then continued to demand a date with the teller and, placing the shotgun under his chin, stated that if he didn't get a date for that night with the teller by the time he counted ten, he would kill himself. In full view of all the customers, employees, and the police officer, he counted to ten and fired the shotgun held under his chin. The results were very final and very spectacular. After a critique of the situation with the officer and employees of the bank, the negotiating team tried to determine, with the help of consulting psychologists and psychiatrists, how to deal with this type of situation and predict the subject's action. Why did this subject kill himself, while others in similar cases allow themselves to be talked out of the situation? Professional people were asked what signs to look for to predict an emotionally disturbed person's actions. How can you tell when one person will commit suicide or kill another, and another person will be talked out of the same threatened course of action? It soon became obvious that there were no answers to the questions, and there were no guarantees that any attempt to dissuade a person from a threatened act would be successful. Police officers looking for the signs of a person "telegraphing" his intended actions have to categorize every emotionally disturbed person as capable of inflicting bodily harm or death upon himself or others. The short time he deals with an emotionally disturbed person in a highly volatile situation does not lend itself to analysis of the person's needs or wants. What it all boils down to is, be careful.

Sometimes negotiating with a person can be initially successful, only to have friends or relatives get into the act and spoil the whole trend of the conversation. Police were called to the scene of a private house by an excited woman who said her twenty-two-year-old son was throwing furniture around, breaking windows, and generally attempting to wreck the place. By the time the police had arrived, the subject had barricaded himself in his bedroom and armed himself with a 2-foot-long machete, threatening everyone to stay away from him. The first officer at the scene began a dialogue with the subject, found that he was probably drunk or mentally disturbed, and requested the negotiating team. Negotiators arrived but did not interfere; the initial police officer was able to get along with subject, and eventually the police officer was on the verge of convincing the man to surrender. As often happens in family disturbances, the mother, who called the police in the first place, now got into the act when she realized that her son was about to be apprehended and led away to a hospital for psychiatric examination. A whole new set of problems evolved, resulting in a tug-of-war between the mother and the police, with her son in the middle. Then a dialogue had to be established with the mother so that she would not end up in the same ward as her son. The situation finally calmed, but the idea of never trusting the relatives of a subject or the alleged victim in a family disturbance was reinforced in the negotiating team's mind.

The gathering of intelligence to deal with a high crisis situation can sometimes be very difficult. Recently, police were called to a large hospital complex and informed that there was a man on the eighteenth floor armed with a bomb and holding a hostage.

When negotiators arrived, they found that between 3:30 and 5:30 AM the man had made eleven phone calls from various parts of the hospital to various switchboards in the hospital complex, threatening to blow up the hospital with a bomb, jump off the eighteenth floor, and/or kill the hostage he held. The reasons given in the various phone calls were that his wife had left him or that his wife had died in the hospital. Attempting to gather all the information from the various persons who had received the calls during the two-hour period became the main job of the negotiating team. While police searched the hospital for the individual, the main switchboard was manned by the negotiating team in hopes that the man would call again. The thought of a man, obviously disturbed, armed with a bomb in a hospital crowded with patients was disconcerting to say the least. Attempting to get a quick "handle" on the subject's problems so that he could be effectively dealt with was of prime necessity. The situation became an exercise of speedy interviews and background checks on the individual, who had identified himself to one of the nurses answering the phone. Finally, at 9:00 AM, the subject was found in a phone booth and subdued. No weapons or bomb were found, and he confessed that the main reason for his actions was that his wife had left him, and he wanted to gain her sympathy. After it was all over, the members of the negotiating team had time to sit back and evaluate their actions. They were amazed at the amount of information about the subject they had gathered in such a short time, which probably would have been extremely valuable in dealing with the individual if he had not been caught.

Hostage negotiations, that is, actually negotiating with the holder of a hostage for some concession on his part, are the name of the game. It is a give-and-take operation; however, there does not have to be a hostage involved for some type of negotiation to take place. On a cold February night negotiators were called to a bridge where a young girl had climbed the railing and was threatening to jump into the water over 100 feet below. Attempts to communicate were made, and finally a limited dialogue with the girl was established by one of the negotiators. All attempts to learn why the girl was threatening suicide were fruitless, so the negotiating team attempted to convince the girl that she was cold, uncomfortable, and would be better off leaving her precarious perch. After two hours, she finally accepted one glove to keep the hand warm that was clutching the cold steel support of the bridge. After awhile, she accepted another glove, and the negotiators were able to move closer. Finally, an officer convinced her that she was cold enough to accept his jacket. Seeing him standing there shivering apparently convinced her to accept his jacket, and, while she was being handed the garment, officers grabbed her and brought her off the bridge. The slow process of negotiating was obviously successful, only this time the subject was being convinced to *accept* things rather than to give them up.

Negotiations sometimes are dangerous, but most of the time the danger can be recognized and its direction pinpointed. However, sometimes outside activity can be very disconcerting to the negotiators Not long ago, negotiators were called to the scene of a burglary where three perpetrators were trapped on the roof by police. The scene was surrounded by officers, and an attempt was made to convince the subjects to surrender and climb down from the roof. While this was taking place, the negotiators came under sniper fire from the rooftop of an adjoining apartment building. In spite of this roadblock thrown in the path of negotiating, the three burglars were convinced to leave the roof. Their unknown benefactor, who attempted to put a crimp in the negotiations, was never apprehended. It is obvious that critiques of incidents such as these can be interesting, informative, and of great value to any agency if they are candid and the officers involved accept criticism of their mistakes without feeling insulted. If an agency will allow interested members of a neighboring department to be present and a reciprocal agreement is established, many more officers involved in negotiating can benefit from each incident.

THE REST OF THE AGENCY AND THE PUBLIC

One of the best ways for a new negotiator to reinforce his confidence is to lecture to other members of the agency about the policies, procedures, and the role of negotiators. If a scheduled

In-Service Training Program is in effect, negotiating should be added to the curriculum. The lecturers should be able to get their philosophy across to the officers and field the resulting questions, thereby alerting the agency to a new way of approaching a police problem.

Lectures should not be limited to the department but broadened to include the public, especially the business segment of the community that may be involved in hostage situations. These lectures can be of great public relations value but also valuable to the agency in other ways. For example, as a result of hostage lectures to some banks, it became evident that bank employees were not triggering hold-up alarms while the perpetrators were inside the bank but were waiting for the stick-up men to exit before setting off the alarm. In many cases the bank camera, coupled with the alarm, did not photograph anything but an empty bank floor. When questioned regarding this procedure during hostage lectures, some banking institutions, both officially and unofficially, blamed efficient, rapid police response to the scene for this attitude of the employees. The employees felt that police, because they could get to the scene so quickly, would contain the perpetrators inside the bank, resulting in a hostage situation such as that recently publicized in movies and on television. The lecturers were able to convince the bank employees of the error of their ways, and now at least photographs should result from alarms triggered during stick-ups.

The local media should be made aware of the existence of a trained negotiating team, and all information considered to be eligible for release regarding the policies of the agency should be made available to the public. Administrators of agencies will be pleasantly surprised at the positive reaction of the press and the public to the idea of negotiation. Even if the negotiators are never used, the comparatively small amount of time invested in the project cannot help but bear some fruit. I urge all to get involved.

APPENDICES

APPENDIX I

THE COMMISSIONER's order disseminating the Nassau County Police Department's policy on hostage/barricade situations was originally issued in 1974 but had to be updated in 1976 and 1977 after experience dictated a need for further clarification of media relationship and as organizational changes took place.

HEADQUARTERS

POLICE DEPARTMENT, COUNTY OF NASSAU

COMMISSIONER'S ORDER   MINEOLA, NEW YORK

NUMBER 21   APRIL 18, 1977

Hostages/Barricade Situation
(Supercedes Commissioner's Order 55 of
1974 and Commissioner's Order 10 of 1976)

A. Duties of Supervising Officers at the Scene of Hostage/Barricade Situations — The overriding principle that should be recognized is THAT THE LIFE OF ANY HOSTAGE IS OF PRIME IMPORTANCE.

  1. Obtain as much information about the situation as possible upon your arrival.

  2. Request the necessary backup as needed such as:
    a. Hostage Negotiators
    b. Precision Firearms Teams
    c. Emergency Equipment (ambulance, lighting, emergency trucks, Command Post Bus, etc.)

  3. Isolate and Secure the area
    a. Evacuation
    b. Traffic
    c. Establish Safe Command Post and designate place for

reporting of other Units.

4. Establish Communications
   a. Designate Channel/Frequency to be used
   b. Request walkie-talkies from other Commands
5. Caution all personnel on overreaction
   a. Firearms Discipline is crucial — don't fire unless your life or somebody else's life is endangered.
6. Do not become involved in in-depth negotiations if such can be avoided; recognize that the first contact is critical.
   a. Await arrival of trained negotiators; however, if negotiations have begun, allow them to continue.
   b. Remember all conversations with subject so as to relate all such to negotiators.
   c. Be guided by these principles:
      1) Have all Units responding to scene advised as to who is in charge, location of Command Post, and ground rules of situation, especially Firearms discipline. Establish a *safe* area for Units to report and broadcast any danger area.
      2) Time is on your side — slow everything down. Do not rush! Some incidents have lasted for days!
      3) If negotiations have started, remember — weapons are *not* negotiable!
7. As situation develops:
   a. Establish inner and outer perimeters — allow only negotiators and Precision Firearms Teams inside the inner perimeter. Establish Command Post in safe, convenient area between the outer and inner perimeters.
   b. Outer perimeter will restrain and divert crowd and traffic — all civilian movement into outer perimeter is to be eliminated.
   c. Supervising Officers of responding Units shall report to Command Post. Large-scale response of personnel should be to a separate staging area.
   d. Communications between inner perimeter and Command Post shall have first priority. Communications

with the staging area shall be maintained by the Command Post.

e. Overall Command of the Operation shall be from Command Post.

f. Responding detectives shall be assigned to gather intelligence, regarding the subject and reasons for his actions, from the following sources:
   1. Family
   2. Neighbors
   3. Friends
   4. Clergy

g. Designate a Supervising Officer as a Media Liaison Officer — An area should be designated as a Press Center inside the outer perimeter and liaison established between the Command Post and the media through the designated Officer.

h. All relatives, friends, and neighbors, shall be limited to access to Outer Command Post only. Overall Commander shall be advised of their presence.

i. The situation may warrant that all communications be established by walkie-talkie — request enough radios to the Command Post to supply all Units. Use plain language — locations and identity of speakers — do not establish Post numbers or numerically designated areas; this may confuse communications.

j. Request Crime Scene Search Unit personnel and request that photographs be taken all during the operation, not only after it is over. These photographs can be of value for both court presentation and future training.

k. Request Command Post Bus. This vehicle affords a Compact Command Post and Communications Center.

l. If special electronic devices such as radios, telephones, television, etc. are thought necessary, request Electronics Unit through Main Office.

m. If hostage (s) is (are) to be moved by subject, make certain that car to be used is equipped with directional tracking equipment.

n. All overt police activity should be outside range of suspect's vision.

o. Keep men on outer perimeter up-to-date in the event hostage (s) is (are) to be moved.

8. Equipment Available — In addition to the normal equipment supplied by the Emergency Services Bureau, the following is available:

a. Command Post Vehicle 1004 (Crime Scene Search Unit) containing Photographic and Crime Scene Equipment — is capable of operation as a mobile Command Post — can be covered with bullet-resistant bomb blankets on hooks — is equipped with bullet-proof glass — has radios on all 7 Low Band frequencies plus both UHF walkie-talkie frequencies and Air Bureau/ Marine Bureau frequency — also 110 volts and air conditioning.

b. Command Post Bus 2484 (Emergency Services Bureau) containing stationery and supplies for long-term operation, toilet facilities, 110/220 volts with radios on all Low Band frequencies plus both walkie-talkie frequencies and Air Bureau/Marine Bureau frequency — air conditioned — can be equipped with 5 telephone numbers.

c. Directional Finding Equipment (Electronics Unit) 5 tracking magnetic transmitters can be affixed to hostage cars — one voice transmitter — three (3) tracking receivers, one capable of airborne operation.

d. Miscellaneous wireless microphones, miniature and full-size tape recorders suitable for 6 hours uninterrupted operation. (Electronics Unit)

e. Night Vision Device (Photography Unit) can be used with or without camera.

f. Shotguns/Sniper Rifles/Tear Gas — will be brought to the scene by the Bureau of Special Operations and used by their trained personnel.

g. Specially equipped Hostage Cars.

B. Established Department Procedure in Hostage Situations

1. The overall Command of a hostage situation shall be the responsibility of the highest ranking officer present, in accord with Article 15, Rule 1, Subdivision 1, of the Rules and Regulations.

2. Prolonged Hostage negotiation shall be conducted by those members specifically trained for that function.

3. The Commanding Officer of the overall operation shall maintain direct contact with the negotiators and the Supervising Officer of the Precision Firearms Teams for the purpose of guidance and decision making.

4. Firearms (unless to protect life) or tear gas shall *not* be used without consent of the Commanding Officer of the Operation and only after consultation with the negotiators.

5. No members of the Force, other than negotiators or Precision Firearms Team members, shall be allowed in the Inner perimeter — strict fire discipline shall be maintained.

6. Liaison with the policy-making, ranking Officers outside the Inner perimeter shall be maintained by the Commanding Officer at the scene.

7. If necessary, liaison with other governmental agencies shall be arranged and maintained by the Outer perimeter Command Post.

8. If tear gas is to be used, provide for masks and fire department equipment.

9. Identified representatives of the media shall be allowed inside the Outer perimeter only for gaining access to the Press Center. Media representatives who refuse to remain in the Press Center should be kept outside the Outer perimeter. The Media Liaison Officer should contact the Public Information Office and identify himself as the member at the scene who will release information and

who can be contacted for information. No information regarding the incident will be released without the consent of the Commanding Officer at the scene and only through the Media Liaison Officer. If Public Information Office is at scene, he is Media Relations Officer.

No interviews will be conducted until the situation has been declared ended or sufficiently under control. Hostage Negotiators shall be consulted regarding any interview to be given if negotiations are still in progress.

10. The most obvious obstacle in obtaining a workable and agreeable procedure for handling prolonged hostage situations is the displacing of those uniformed members, first at the scene and inside the Inner perimeter, with the Teams, for the maintenance of firearms discipline. It is also absolutely necessary that those members negotiating with the suspect be consulted and no outside action be contemplated without their knowledge.

11. The negotiators shall be called to the scene of *all situations* where they may be of use — not only when the holding of hostages is known, but also when there are no hostages, but only a barricaded subject. Hostage Team may be summoned:

First: By telephone, if readily accessible, to Supervising Officer, Communications Bureau*

*   *   *

a) 535-4320
b) 535-4141
c) "911" Supervisor calling to identify himself and request to be connected to Communications Bureau Superior Officer.

Second: Request through Radio Transmission to Radio Dispatcher

---

*Purpose of above to limit monitoring of radio request by unauthorized persons and excessive response to scene by unauthorized Department personnel and Units and civilians.

APPENDIX II

T HE FOLLOWING is an outline used in 1975 by the Nassau County Police Department Hostage Negotiating Team to train a team from a neighboring Department.

HOSTAGE NEGOTIATION TRAINING OUTLINE
I. *INTRODUCTION*
   A. *INTRODUCTION OF MEMBERS OF NASSAU COUNTY POLICE*
      1. We are here to give basics received from New York City and subsequent training.
      2. We hope to stimulate your thoughts.
      3. We don't have all the answers.
      4. You may have more questions when we are done than when we started.
   B. *GROUND RULES FOR DISCUSSION*
      1. Interrupt at any time with questions and statements.
      2. Basic outline of what is to come — don't get insulted in role playing (short talk on role playing). Self-criticism.
   C. *HISTORY OF HOSTAGE NEGOTIATION IN NAS-SAU COUNTY*
      1. Seminar in Washington in September 1974.
      2. School in New York City in November/December 1974 Most Experience. (We have kept most of what was taught but not all.)
      3. At least monthly training ever since
         a. Unit is mostly self-trained
         b. Psychological help
      4. Makeup of Nassau Unit
         a. 22 members, etc.

D. *SUFFOLK PROGRAM — TO MAKE IT WORK*
 1. We can only scratch the surface.
 2. You must take it from here in training.
 3. You must believe in it.
 4. You have to have acceptance from other Department members.
 5. Get your psychological counselor involved.
 6. Don't let "SWAT" influence your thinking.

E. *PROBLEMS YOU WILL HAVE*
 1. Other members not believing in the theory of negotiation.
 2. Obtaining cooperation from other commands.
 3. Establishing a workable procedure in the Department.
 4. Obtaining a firm department policy and having it disseminated. (New York vs California Policy on Negotiation.)
 5. Obtaining permission to train at least monthly.

F. *TRAINING*
 1. Self-training is important — self-criticism
    a. It holds unit together — bond is established.
    b. Promotes interest.
    c. Everyone learns in role playing.
    d. It is important that each negotiator knows *strong* and *weak* points of each other.

G. *LIAISON WITH OTHER UNITS*
 1. Invite them to your training as observers.
 2. Observe their training or at least have them explain their function as it applies to you.
 3. Give lectures in Department schools.
 4. Units involved:
    a. Precision firearms team
    b. Assault team
    c. Electronics Section
    d. Detectives
    e. Emergency equipment
    f. Uniform force

H. *NEGOTIATION BASICS*
  1. No mystique — most cops do it every day.
     a. Family disturbances.
     b. Neighborhood feuds.
     c. Suicide attempts.
     d. Actual hostage/barricade situations.
  2. Policy must be — the hostage's life is prime importance.
  3. Slow Down!!
  4. You may be dealing with one or a combination of the following situations:
     a. The criminal — escape from crime, etc.
     b. The mentally disturbed — various types of anxiety and stress problems.
     c. The loose-knit group — jails, civil disturbances.
     d. The organized group — radicals.
  5. Try and recognize the type you are dealing with.
     a. The criminal is the easiest to deal with.
     b. The mental problem may be a suicide attempt.
     c. The loose knit group is easier than the organized group if rapid action is taken before a leader is chosen.
  6. In future role playing you should touch on all.
I. *NASSAU EXPERIENCE*
  1. Fortunate in having caliber of people involved.
  2. Have been involved in five situations:
     a. Bethpage — man with shotgun — wife
     b. Mineola — man with shotgun — phony
     c. Locust Valley — A & R
     d. Roosevelt — man with shotgun — girl friend
     e. Baldwin — man with machete — no hostage
     No negotiation in any — yet still maintains interest of personnel.
  3. We also were called on suicide attempt.
  4. Many of members have prior experience.
J. I am going to turn you over to other members. Remember in next few days —

1. Don't blow your cool.
2. If you can be reached because of thin skin — you will be useless.
3. Agree or disagree with us — but think about it.
4. Take what we give and go on from there.
5. Repeat — Slow Down!!

II. *HOSTAGE NEGOTIATION THEORY*

   A. Keen interest started for most Police Departments shortly after "Munich Episode" at Olympic games, (1972) and New York City "Gilroy," John and Al's incident (1973).

   B. Negotiation Definition: To treat or bargain with others in order to reach an agreement.
(Not just to get into position to neutralize.)

   C. To *believe* in the "Negotiation" concept is most important to a successful negotiation.
(You will have many dissenters to the program)

DON'T WEAKEN!!

   D. Types of persons who take hostages:

     1. Professional criminal — wants money or escape and is usually easiest to deal with.

     2. Mentally ill or psychotic persons (latter being most dangerous). Very difficult to determine between the two.

SIGNS OF PSYCHO

     a. *Frustration* — wanting something and not being able to get it. The end result of this is usually aggression and creative thinking (bomb maker).

     b. *Conflict* — wanting something and not wanting it at the same time. (example: love and hate) Conflict breeds a sense of power — no one noticed him before — now he's the center of attraction. He may want to go or stay, indecisive — will have difficulty coping with the situation he created.

     c. *Anxiety* — This comes from overabundance of frustration and conflict — all people experience it,

however, the psycho has too much. Hostage situations of all types are loaded with anxiety — you
should always attempt to decrease this and not add
to it!! Be Calm!! Listen!!

d. Excessive anxiety tends to make a person extremely
sensitive (aware sharp senses) try to keep this person in a problem-solving atmosphere to reduce his
awareness. (How can I help? Would you like to
leave?)

e. Treatments of Awareness and Anxiety:
(1) Time is most effective. Anxiety decreases with
passage of time. (Don't put a time limit on
your negotiations. May last for days.)
(2) Sleep reduces anxiety.
(3) Sex reduces anxiety.
(4) One of negotiators prime functions is to treat
and release anxiety. (Don't let the already
full bowl overflow.)

3. Loose groups (Jail situation — Prisoners grab a guard)
a. If you can get to this situation before a leader sur-
faces and plans are made, generally within one
hour you can deal effectively by immediate actions
and proper use of force (otherwise, you must
negotiate as you would with the individual) .

4. Organized group or terrorists (very difficult to deal
with)
a. He may be convinced *dying* is to show belief in his
cause.
b. He rationalizes his behavior and feels he's "helping
mankind" or his oppressed group.
c. In these cases, his resolve to die for his cause may
diminish with passage of time. (As in John and
Al's — they asked for doctor.) Once again, "Time"
is so important.
d. In any event, once this type kills a hostage during
negotiations to "Prove his point" (Here's a body,
you have a half hour before I throw out next one).

You now must assault before next killing in effort to save those remaining hostages.

Once he kills one — he is likely to kill more.

e. Basic approaches to hostage situation:

   (1) Assault.

   (2) Selected sniper fire.

   (3) Use of chemical agents.

   (4) Contain and negotiate. (Remember you can go from number four to any of the others — but it's not the same in reverse.)

f. The Negotiators Role:

   (1) He should be a mature individual with a calming approach.

   (2) Good talker — preferably Detective personnel who have experience in interrogation, interviews, etc.

   (3) Not thin skinned or susceptible to ethnic slurs, etc. Nonargumentive approach.

   (4) He should not portray himself as the ultimate decision maker (most people accept the "I have to see my boss" syndrome).

    This will be a good stalling ploy.

   (5) Be firm and sure but not overpowering.

   (6) Don't be a "pawn" and agree with everything. You must "negotiate" for everything. (Even cigarettes, etc., try to get something in return — lower gun, give medicine to hostage, etc.)

   (7) Let holder know you want to listen and help. Be sincere (and mean it).

   (8) Let him talk so you can identify his problems.

   (9) Offer him realistic alternatives to solving his problems.

 (10) Negotiator should be prepared and willing to be at times unarmed while near the holder (he probably will demand this) he may even demand that you undress to a degree.

(11) Count and have recorded any shots fired by holder.

(12) Determine type(s) of weapon(s) he has (bomb, etc.) .

(13) Slow everything down ("Time is your most effective tool") .

(14) Get the "John Wayne" — "SWAT" syndrome completely out of your thoughts.   (It shows.) If he senses your motive for talking to him is strictly "assault" or "jump him," you will not reach a "transference."

(15) Reinforce good things done by holder by agreeing with him.

(16) Remember the holder is the "Star" of the show and he knows it — play to him — avoid conversation with the hostages.

(17) Avoid bringing family or loved ones, clergy, etc., to scene.   (These are people psycho is playing to.)   If they could help him, he might not be here.

(18) Be aware he might ask for someone to be brought to him merely to kill them before killing self.

(19) Remember many hostage situations are elaborate attempts to commit suicide. A safe basic assumption is to consider them homicidal.
(Transference is the *automatic* relationship that forms between people.)

(20) Time is the most important factor when trying to reach this "transference" feeling — As a general rule, the longer he spends with hostages, the less likely he is to take hostage's life, because they become acquainted and develop feelings for one another.   (This transference is what you're aiming for between you and him.)

(21) While allowing this transference of feelings to

take place — the passage of time allows Police to plan for different eventualities and for the holder to make mistakes.

(22) Remember practically all demands are negotiable but two:

(a) We don't give him weapons.

(b) We don't give him additional hostages. (However, it may become necessary to supply an unarmed driver for a vehicle.)

(23) Whenever something is given to him, even as small as a cigarette, make it obvious to him you are putting yourself out to help him.

(24) Assume all of these persons are homicidal — don't take unnecessary chances — with a true psychopath, negotiations probably won't be effective. Assault is the only way.

(25) If assault is to be considered — 0530 is best time (fresh troops) ; also after sex.

(26) If you can't make it with him — don't push it. (It's not a "you," "him," "win," "lose" situation.) Send in another member of team. It's a team effort.

(27) If he tells you to get out — Get Out.

(28) You will find a strong bond and close relationship and *esprit de corps* forming within the hostage unit.

(29) Find out if any promises have been made to him before your arrival.

(30) What does he look like, name, etc., background, relatives, etc.? What's he wearing?

(31) Who are hostages? —— What do they look like?

(32) SLOW DOWN!! EVERYTHING!!

(33) Remember the first 10 minutes of negotiations are most dangerous — don't unnecessarily expose yourself.

(34) Try to read his body language — shifting, un-

easy, calm, happy, etc.

(35) After First contact, *Let Him Talk.*

(36) Has anyone else talked to him?

(37) Gather intelligence on him before making contact, if possible.

g. Ways to Negotiate

    (1) Telephone, bullhorn.

    (2) Face-to-face contact is most effective but take cover (play peek-a-boo). No need to face him directly in the open.

    (3) Sole purpose of negotiations is for the holder to deal with authority — the negotiator should not be afraid to say no and should not become a pawn.

    (4) Approximately 5 to 10 feet is the best distance to have the desired effect on a person's feelings in a negotiation (transference).

    (5) Three feet and under is his "Intimate Space" — you then become a threat — (Restaurant Experiment.)

h. REMEMBER — Three principles to crisis intervention:

    (1) Negotiator should form a relationship indicating he is willing to listen.

    (2) Attempt to let holder talk and identify his problem.

    (3) The Negotiator should offer alternatives to solve holders problems.

i. How to Start Negotiations:

    (1) Introduce yourself as the Negotiator — tell him your name "Joe Green."

    (2) Don't give him a big story about your rank, job, etc. unless he asks specific questions.

    (3) If asked if you are a Police Officer, tell truth. It's easy enough for him to determine this fact.

    (4) Tell him you're there to help him and *listen.*

(5) If no conversation ensues, remain silent, he
will respond eventually.

(6) Use noncommittal verbalization — Example:
Uh, Huh, Really, etc. This tends to imply
interest.

(7) Don't try to argue him into negotiation.
When he's ready, he'll talk.

(8) Don't go into this with a "big canned pitch"
in mind. Play each step and sentence to his
problem as he relates to you.

(9) Remember no two situations will be alike;
therefore, there can be no standard format for
negotiation talk.

(10) Slow everything down and speak to him with
confidence.

(11) Show sincerity in your words; believe what
you're saying and don't lie about anything he
can pin you down on.

(12) Remember don't talk to hostages — he's got
the grandstand and wants it that way.

III. *HOSTAGE/BARRICADE/SUICIDE*

Success in each phase of the program will depend a great deal
on:

Intelligence—Communication—Coordination

A. Duties of First Officer at Scene:

1. Attempt to learn what type situation or incident you
are dealing with.

Is there actually a hostage?
Is there a crime involved?
Is there a mental aided?
Is the Holder in possession of weapons?
Do you have a suicide attempt?

2. Get all information regarding your incident out to
Communications Bureau immediately by radio, phone,
or any method available.

3. Contain and isolate area — seal off area to vehicle and

pedestrian traffic.

4. Evacuate where necessary and safe.

5. Establish perimeter to prevent escape from containment (containment slide).

6. Establish temporary command point (PD?) until a command post can be set up — notify all responding assistance where to report and how to get there safely.

7. If the first officer at scene starts to negotiate and is accepted by the holder

   a. Let him talk as long as things are going our way.

   b. Don't promise something you cannot produce — always stall by saying you have to talk to a higher authority (stall). Keep track of anything said to or by the holder.

   c. When starting to talk to a holder, be safe and cautious (slide).

8. Make every effort to learn the ID of holder or any other persons involved.

B. *As Situation Develops*

1. Supervisor should never assign first officer to task that would remove him from availability.

2. Make sure communication is maintained at all cost — (slide) — Firearms discipline must be maintained, don't fire unless your life or someone else's is in immediate danger — then take proper action. Let all concerned know about any shots fired during negotiation.

3. Make sure perimeter is secure and unauthorized persons are kept out. Holder may want to talk to a particular reporter to play up his plight or crusade. Also, the holder may have access to radio or T.V. — If wrong information or information that would serve as intelligence to holder were broadcast, it could set him off.

4. Establish a staging area beyond the perimeter for a Command Post — relatives — off-duty Police Officers — equipment — clergy — medical assistance.

5. Remember, in most situations time is on your side —
   "Slow Down" — some incidents have lasted for days —
   Forget — "SWAT."
6. Have all units responding to scene know who is in
   charge of operation.
7. Responding Detectives should be utilized to gather
   further intelligence regarding the subject and possible
   reasons for his actions.
8. If possible, have Police Photographer taking photos
   of operation while it is in progress — not just at completion — photos could have value later.
9. Don't use tear gas without proper equipment available (Masks — Fire Department). If an assault is
   necessary, let the trained assault teams do it.
   *DON'T PUT A TIME LIMIT ON ANY SITUA-
   TION.*

IV. *NEGOTIATION TEAM*

A. Upon arrival of Negotiation Team, they must first get
   briefed on the situation at hand — go over all the intelligence available — then confer among each other the
   most favorable way to start the actual negotiating and
   who to use (Make up a game plan).
   Is the holder of an ethnic background that we have available?
   Would it be advisable to use someone of the same or
   similar background?

B. Check with the supervisor in charge of the situation,
   make suggestions relative to the possibility of being able
   to talk the holder out.

C. Check and double check to see that your communications
   with the Command Post and Precision Firearm Teams
   are all working properly.

D. After a determination has been made as to who will start
   the negotiation, the number two man will take care of
   communications and recording what is said.

E. The rest of the team members will be involved as back-ups or replacements for one and two.

They will continue to gather intelligence and feed one and two.

They will endeavor to contain the holder with methods such as tying door handles to prevent holder from any quick action type door opening. Make effort to obtain keys to building where holder is.

F. During the in-depth negotiations, the negotiator may make a deal for — booze — radio — T.V. — food — cigarettes — or even the possibility of drugs. As in all phases of the negotiations, make the holder think he is being done a big favor by granting him certain items — he must also give, in order to receive, although his giving may be just a promise.

Use as a stalling tactic the fact you cannot grant him the item he wants until you check with higher authority.

In the event there is need for a rescue operation to remove wounded or trapped person — *NO ONE SHOULD PLAY A HERO ROLE.*

The time spent waiting for the proper equipment to effect such an operation may save additional injuries.

Use a rescue ambulance properly equipped to get between holder and those trapped.

G. *WEAPONS AND POLICE OFFICERS ARE NEVER NEGOTIABLE UNDER ANY CIRCUMSTANCES.*

A West Coast Police Department has in their rules: "A Police Officer who negotiates for either of the above items has terminated his own employment."

H. Remember one of the main reasons for slowing everything down is to wear down the holder and save your hostages — we can escalate a situation at any time, but it is very difficult to de-escalate.

I. During negotiations, it is advisable for the talker to be unarmed and possibly able to prove it to the holder. We are told by the psychologist that once a transference has taken place and we have face-to-face negotiations, the holder may ask the talker to prove he is unarmed and make him undress.

J. The Command Post policy must be known by all. Should a decision be made to strike or neutralize the holder, the negotiator would try to maneuver the holder into a position where the Precision Firearm Teams could get a shot at him — or at this time the talker may secrete a weapon (small automatic or Derringer) on himself and make the strike when possible.

K. If the holder has a group of hostages and sets a time limit of for example: 10 minutes — we will continue to try and talk him out of it. If we fail and he kills the first hostage, our policy is to set a full assault in motion as soon as possible to prevent him from killing number two. This means, of course, that all negotiations are off; however, even after the first hostage has been killed, we will continue, if possible, to talk to the holder only as a diversion for the assault team or to possibly make the strike ourselves.

L. A negotiator will not exchange himself for a hostage; however, if an escape auto is dealt for, the negotiator may, at the request of the holder (not voluntarily), become the driver, thus becoming a hostage. If this occurs, we have a caravan set up in case holder changes his location.

M. Prior to any transference, a negotiator will not put himself in a position whereby he will become an additional hostage. Remember, the possibility of letting the holder go in order to save a hostage *does exist*.

V. *ROLE PLAYING*
  A. Let emotions surface.
  B. Keep mistakes in mind for critique.
  C. This is the best training and should continue.
  D. Sessions — divide into four teams, pick your own Talker One, Talker Two. Change over during session.

1. *Telephone*

   Man in own home — threatened neighbors with shot-gun about parking in front of his house — fired shot in air — has been acting strange in past — wife and two kids may be in house — aim is to effect safe entry by Police, safe exit of wife and kids or surrender of subject — Police have not attempted communication. Subject: James Miller — wife, Gloria — kids, Tommy and Ann.

2. *Bullhorn/Radio*

   Same situation only no phone — subject has fired one shot at Police car — aim is to get subject to accept radio by getting his confidence with bullhorn — instruction to him on use of radio — final aim — safe exit by wife and kids and surrender of subject. No prior communication by Police.

3. *Telephone/Voice*

   Situation — robbery of bar — subject runs out of premises — Police Officer is fired upon — returns fire — subject runs into real estate office — one male working in office — subject fires at Police and has threatened to kill hostage if Police attempt to enter office — subject is unknown male, white.

4. *Voice*

   Situation — bar near family court — man who is known alcoholic has been told to stay away from wife and kids for good due to wife beating — subject has wife in bar alone with him and threatens to kill her and himself unless he can see kids every day — kids are in car outside with aunt. He has threatened suicide in past — subject: male, white, Joe Barnes; wife: Joan; kids: Joseph and Jane. All bar patrons forced to leave by holder — he threatened to kill case worker who recommended court action — wife is problem for negotiators.

5. *Voice*

Situation — male, black militant has been slipped a gun by unknown person while being held on a robbery charge in court detention area — he holds Sheriff's Deputy also has his gun — threatens to kill unless he is provided with car to airport and traveling money — says he will kill himself before going back to jail. Holder: Jerry Brown, male, black, 26 years — prior robbery record.

6. *Bullhorn/Phone/Voice*

Situation — 3 males escaping from prisoner van hold hostages in a pizza shop — armed with knives — they want car and 15 minute start — hold Police Officer when he tries to negotiate — use his gun to kill first negotiator after conning him inside — no apparent leader of group at first.

7. *Voice*

Situation — unknown male, states he has bomb and is going to blow up hospital building — he is in first floor coffee shop — he wants Governor brought to scene to lead investigation into sloppy hospital practice that resulted in wife Marie's death 10 years ago — he says he is engineer and was in army demolition during World War II — he has attache case.

APPENDIX III

FIGURES 1a and 1b depict the variation in size of an inner and outer perimeter depending on the weapon of the subject.

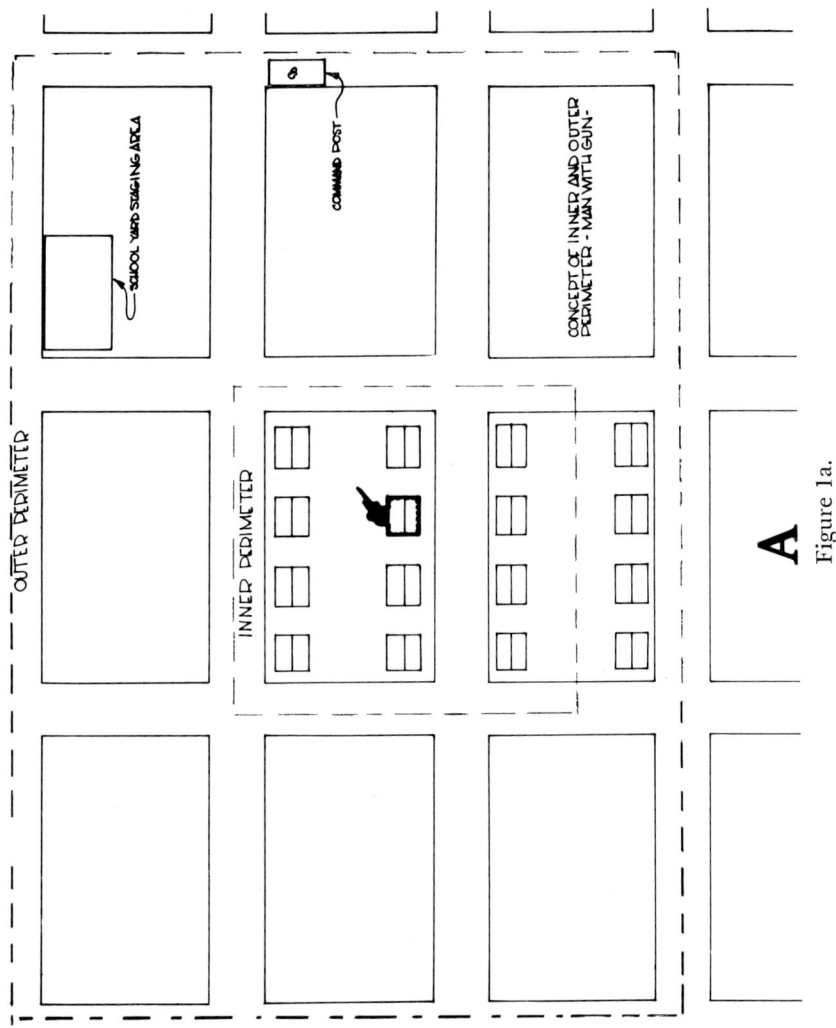

Figure 1a.

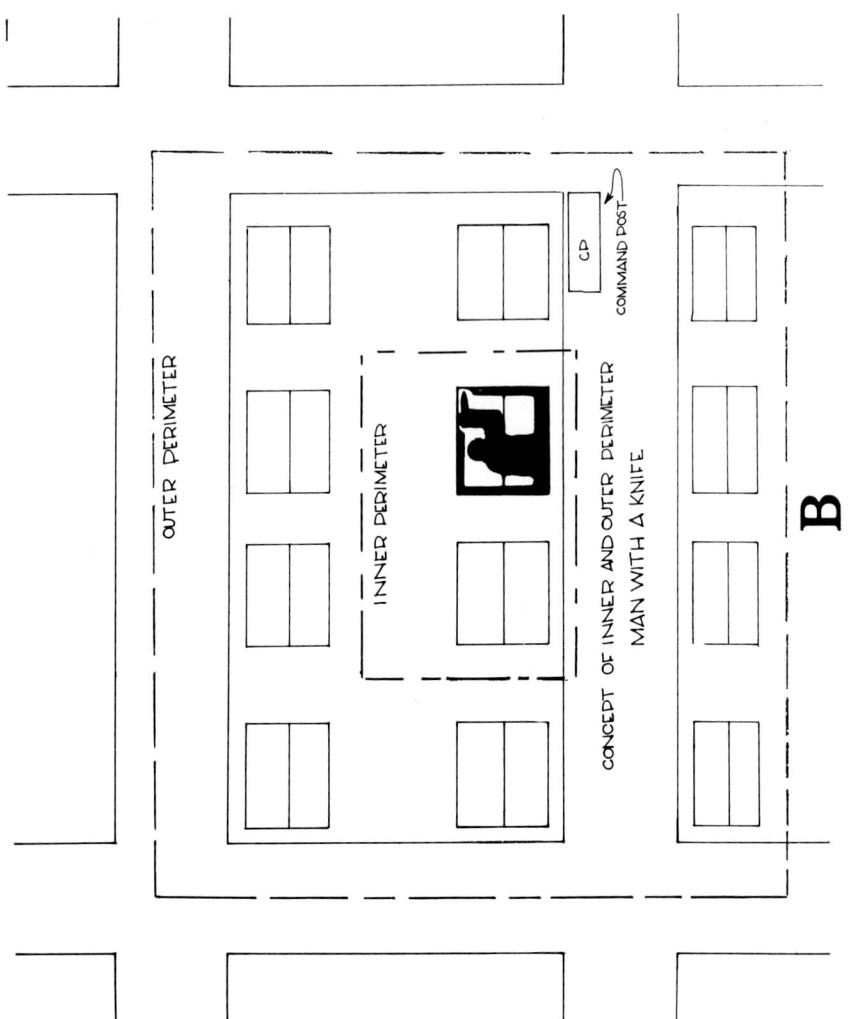

CONCEPT OF INNER AND OUTER PERIMETER
MAN WITH A KNIFE

Figure 1b.

APPENDIX IV

Description and photographs of recommended electronic devices.

SURVEILLANCE KIT

Used in conjunction with a body-worn, 1-watt miniature transmitter, this system receives any transmitted voice signals from the negotiator wearing the transmitter.

The system also has the capability of recording, simultaneously, the transmitted conversations. A pocket receiver with an earpiece is available for the use of a back-up negotiator. The main receiver is crystal controlled and all parts of the system are capable of operation from either AC or battery power sources.

REMOTE CONTROLLED IGNITION SYSTEM

This device is a remotely controlled ignition shut-off system consisting of a radio transmitter/Digital Tone Encoder and a Radio Receiver/Digital Tone Decoder.

The receiver/decoder system will respond only to the proper tone sequence that is generated by the transmitter/encoder.

Various tone sequences may be generated to perform different functions within the vehicle.

This system consists of four tones simultaneously transmitted and decoded. The absence of any one of these tones will not allow the decoder to respond, thus not permitting the vehicle to be turned off or back on again by an outside source.

The receiver/decoder is installed in the trunk or under the hood of the hostage vehicle, while the transmitter/encoder is carried in the trailing vehicle. Installation time is usually about five minutes when connected with the relay interrupting the hot side of the coil.

A limited range is desirable; however, this system has been tested at distances up to 3 miles.

79

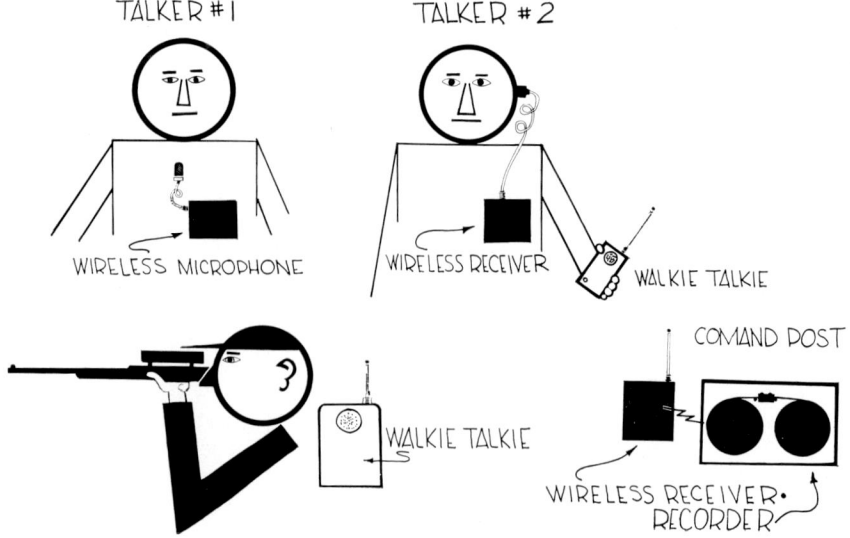

Figure 2.

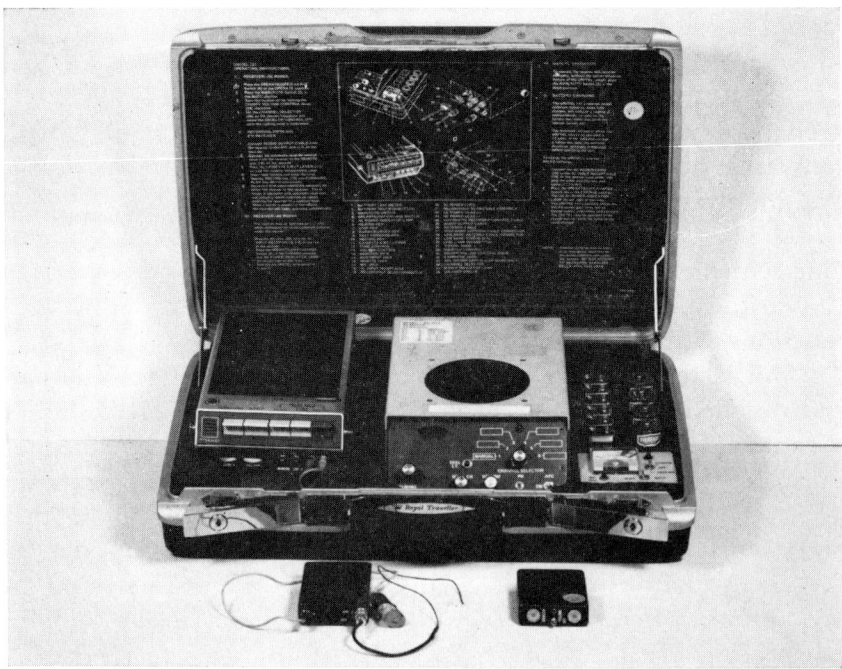

Figure 3. An intelligence system capable of supporting a negotiation session. It contains a cassette recorder and a multi-channel, crystal-controlled receiver. A miniature transmitter and a receiver are in the foreground.

Generally, the system would be installed with the vehicle ignition in the "on" position. When it is desired to disable the vehicle, the transmitter/encoder is activated, thus causing the receiver/decoder to respond to turn the vehicle ignition "off."

The ignition will remain in the off position until it receives another signal from the transmitter/encoder.

Erratic vehicle operation, due to engine problems, can be simulated using this system.

Any available police walkie-talkies can be adapted to this function with the addition of the digital tone encoder/decoder.

This particular system, using VHF walkie-talkies, was designed and built by the Nassau County Police Department Electronics Unit.

50-WATT "CONSTANT ON" VEHICLE TRANSMITTER

A 50-watt "constant on" transmitter with a key-activated control box is mounted in the trunk of the hostage vehicle; the transmitter will transmit any voice conversations within the vehicle to any police vehicle in the vicinity.

Within the control box is a switching arrangement that, once activated, will disengage the normal police radio, activate the hostage radio, and change over the antenna to the hostage radio.

The output frequency of the transmitter is the same as the receive frequency of the standard police radio so that all the cars involved in the hostage situation will be able to hear the conversation within the vehicle.

A sensitive, noise-cancelling microphone was installed in the headliner of the vehicle so that it will pick up the voices of persons occupying both the front seats as well as the rear seats.

When the control box is activated with the key switch, the key is then removed so that the transmitter will not be able to be turned off even if the holder had access to the trunk of the vehicle.

The tested range of this radio configuration is at least one mile.

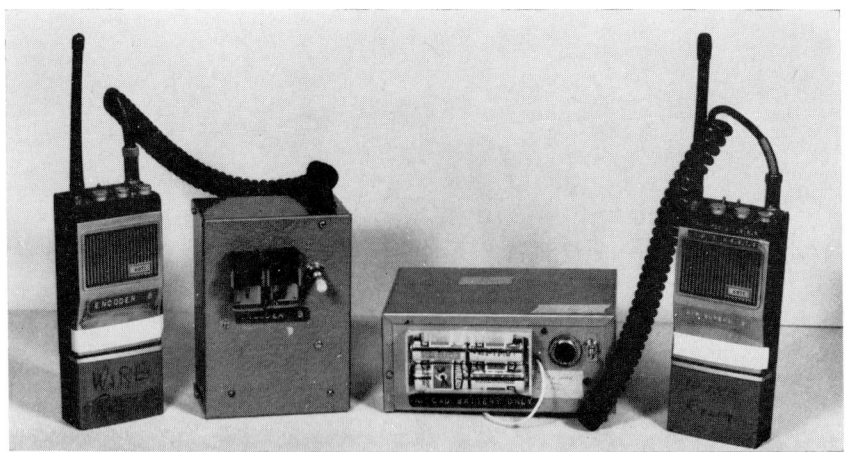

Figure 4. The ignition control device consisting of the encoder with a walkie-talkie, to be carried in the follow-up car, and the decoder attached to its radio, which will be installed in the hostage car.

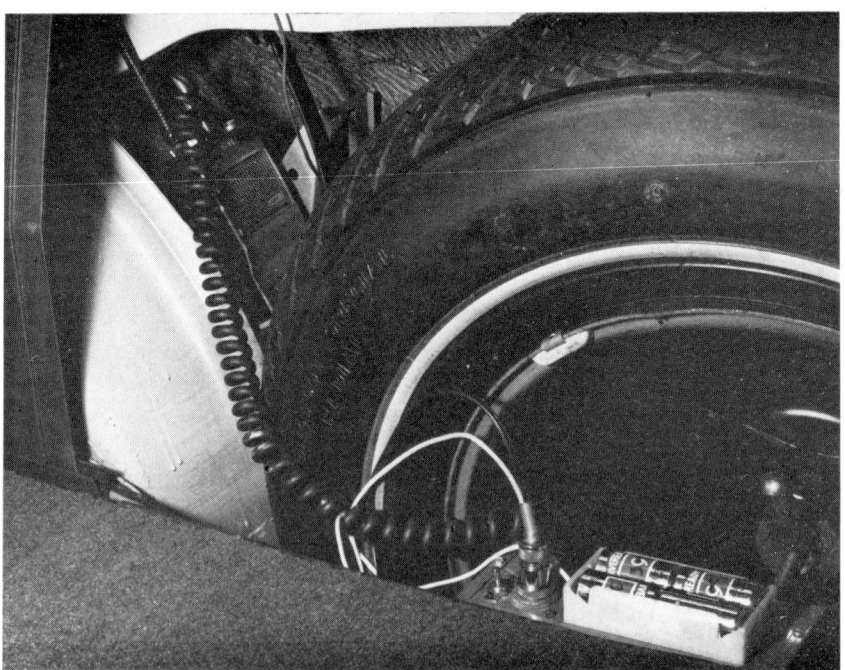

Figure 5. The ignition control device in the trunk of a hostage car, with control wires to the coil running under the floor mats. It also can be placed under the hood if time is a problem.

Figure 6. The key-controlled, constant-on transmitter in the trunk of the hostage car. Microphones are concealed in the headliner.

VEHICLE TRACKING SYSTEM

The vehicle tracking system is used for tracking and locating a vehicle through the use of a miniature transmitter installed on the vehicle.

This system may be used to locate a target from another vehicle and is especially effective when used in a helicopter.

The system provides a method of maintaining constant surveillance on a subject vehicle from a discrete distance without the necessity of constant visual contact.

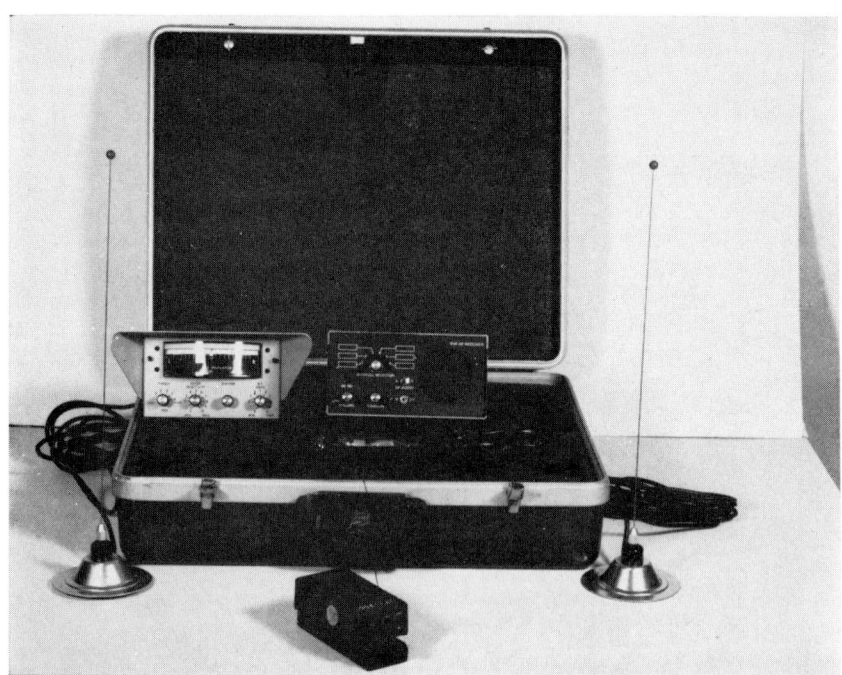

Figure 7. Electronic direction-tracking system with transmitter in foreground.

Figure 8. Installing the magnetic direction-tracking transmitter to the underside of the hostage car.

APPENDIX V

THESE situations, reported in the language of the media, are typical of the incidents that had to be dealt with in Nassau County, New York during the past few years.

Bethpage, September 19

A twenty-nine-year-old man was arrested in the bedroom of his home after he allegedly threatened a neighbor with a shotgun. After two hours of trying to communicate with the individual, bullhorn and telephone were utilized by the Police Hostage Negotiating Team, an entry was made into the house by bullet-proof-vest-clad police officers, and the subject was arrested. An unloaded, single shot 12-gauge shotgun was found in the bedroom. No injuries were reported.

Mineola, October 23

One hundred and fifty police officers, some armed with automatic weapons and wearing bullet-proof vests, with the assistance of hovering helicopters, searched an apartment complex for a man with a shotgun. A Police Hostage Negotiating Team, after an extensive investigation and interview of the complainant involved, called off the search and pronounced it a figment of the woman's imagination. She was removed to the Medical Center for psychiatric examination.

Locust Valley, December 31

Police arrested three New York City men after the 19,000 dollar robbery of the Nassau Trust Company. The ski-masked subjects entered the bank at opening, produced a .45 automatic and a revolver, and forced the manager and four female tellers to aid in their escape. Police, after being summoned to the scene by a silent alarm, exchanged shots with the perpetrators, forcing them back into the bank. An attempt at negotiation with the robbers was made by the police, and in exchange for two of the bank employees, the men were allowed to leave the bank with three women hostages in a car owned by one of the tellers. With one of the robbers driving, the car containing the three female hostages and the three perpetrators left Nassau County and proceeded through Queens County and into Kennedy Airport. A police caravan followed the hostage car from Kennedy Airport into Brooklyn, where the three perpetrators were apprehended on Flatbush Avenue. During the apprehension, one shot was fired and one of the subjects was slightly injured while resisting arrest. None of the hostages were harmed.

Roosevelt, November 18

First Precinct Police, with the assistance of the Hostage Negotiating Team, arrested a Roosevelt man after a prolonged siege at a condemned building on Lakewood Avenue last night. The subject had allegedly held police at bay with a shotgun while holding an unidentified female for over three hours. After repeated attempts to negotiate with the individual, police surreptitiously entered the building through the rear while diverting the subject's attention to the front. He was taken into custody without a struggle. A shotgun was found in the bedroom where the subject had been found with the woman. No injuries were reported.

Baldwin, November 23

A twenty-two-year-old Baldwin man, who held family, neighbors, and police at bay for over two hours last night with a 2-foot-long machete, was finally talked into surrendering by the Police Hostage Negotiating Team. The man, an out-patient from Milburn State Hospital, was taken by police ambulance to the Nassau County Medical Center Psychiatric Ward. No injuries were reported.

East Meadow, January 11

A twenty-two-year-old Uniondale man was charged yesterday

with making threatening phone calls to the Nassau County Medical Center warning that he would blow up the hospital. He also stated to the hospital switchboard that he was on the premises and had taken a hostage. While police and security guards searched the hospital complex, the negotiating team attempted to deal with the subject during subsequent phone calls. The man was spotted by a hospital employee who subdued him and held him for the police. No injuries were reported. The man was arrested for three counts of harassment.

Laurel Hollow, January 29

A member of the Nassau County Police Hostage Negotiating Team convinced a distraught nineteen-year-old Laurel Hollow man to surrender himself to the officer. The youth had barricaded himself in a locked room in his parents' home where the father maintained a sizable gun collection. After over an hour of conversation, the youth surrendered and was removed to South Oaks Hospital in Amityville.

Roslyn, February 24

A fifteen-year-old girl tied up traffic and kept police at a distance for more than an hour last night when she threatened to leap from the Roslyn viaduct into the cold and choppy waters of Hempstead Harbor, 140 feet below. A thirty-three-year-old police officer, who managed to befriend the girl, grabbed her when she reached for a glove he offered her. The girl, who was not identified by the police, was taken to the Nassau County Medical Center for observation. Police say the episode began to unfold at 9:10 PM when a call came to the Sixth Precinct that a girl was threatening to jump from the viaduct. Radio cars, emergency units, marine units, and the Hostage Negotiating Team were dispatched to the area and quickly closed all lanes to traffic until the girl was taken into custody.

Hempstead, February 27

Three burglary suspects were trapped on the roof of the North Franklin Street Restaurant early today for more than an hour be-

fore surrendering, while police said they were still looking for
a sniper who fired at officers from a nearby apartment house.
Police officers apparently startled the burglars inside the restaurant near Jackson Street when responding to alarm about 4:00
AM. The three fled to the roof and did not surrender until after
5:00 AM, at which time more than seventy-five police officers, in-
cluding the Hostage Negotiating Team, Precision Firearms
Teams and other units, surrounded and illuminated the area.
Negotiations with the three men on the roof were hampered by a
sniper who fired three shots from the roof of an adjoining apartment house. The three men were taken into custody after surrendering. The sniper was not apprehended.

Westbury, April 6

Dozens of police armed with shotguns and other special equipment surrounded the home of a knife-wielding man for more than
five hours yesterday before crashing through the front and back
doors and capturing him unharmed. The man was involved in a
similar incident in August when he held off police with a high-
powered rifle. The incident began shortly before 1:30 PM when
two sheriff's deputies were sent to the house to serve an arrest
warrant for assault, which his wife had obtained at Family Court.
The man threatened the deputies with a knife and they withdrew,
summoning the police. The police cordoned off the entire block
and, with the arrival of the Hostage Negotiating Team, made a
series of telephone calls attempting to pursuade him to surrender.
He claimed he had a shotgun as well as a knife and would use
them. At about 3:30 PM, police, armed with shotguns, bullet-
proof vests, and riot shield moved into position and stormed the
premises while the Negotiating Team kept the man engaged in
conversation on the telephone. No injuries were reported.

Lakeview, May 11

Fifth Precinct Police Officers received a call at 9:30 last night.
A male with a shotgun had barricaded himself in a basement on
Smith Street and was holding hostages. Police arrived at the
scene and evacuated adjoining houses and cordoned off the block.

A woman was interviewed, and she stated that her estranged husband had been banging at the front door with a shotgun in his hand and threatening to kill her. She said she attempted to call the police, but the telephone line had been cut, and then heard noises coming from the basement. The police attempted to make contact with the man in the cellar and, after hearing no sounds indicating the cellar was occupied, searched the entire home with the aid of periscopes. The subject was not found, and a notification was broadcast for his arrest.

Levittown, August 15

A former army marksman, who escaped after allegedly terrorizing a nineteen-year-old ex-girlfriend, barricaded himself in his Levittown apartment with a military surplus carbine early yesterday before surrendering to the Nassau County Police Hostage Negotiating Team in a four and a half hour face-to-face confrontation. Two members of the Negotiating Team convinced the subject to lay down a fully loaded .30 caliber army carbine and surrender to them. In the apartment police found an additional fifty rounds of .30 caliber ammunition. The subject was arrested.

East Meadow, August 31

After five hours of perching on the garage roof of his parents' home and threatening to slash his throat with a sheetrock knife if the police came near him, a twenty-five-year-old bus mechanic was finally subdued yesterday after he momentarily fell asleep, awakened, and attempted to crawl back into the house window. Members of the Nassau Police Department Negotiating Team and other officers attempted to persuade him to leave the roof, and he finally crawled back through a broken window, offering no resistance to the officers waiting inside. He was removed to the Medical Center for psychiatric examination.

Baldwin, November 22

A fifty-two-year-old Baldwin Harbor man surrendered to the police after forcing his family from their home at the point of a rifle and then nailing the doors and windows shut. After more than four hours he was talked into surrendering by the Police Hostage Negotiating Team, after repeatedly threatening to kill himself if anyone attempted entry into the premises. He was removed to the Nassau County Medical Center for observation.